To My t.
Monica —
Stay curious
keep seeking
keep an open mind !!

Whatever you are looking
for, you will find !!

Love
Mary Rose Taylor
"Aunt Rose"

TAKE ANOTHER LOOK

You Are Anointed, Appointed,
and Positioned for Victory!

Including A Special Section About The Author

MARY ROSE TRAYLOR

LifeRich Publishing is a registered trademark of The Reader's Digest Association, Inc.

LifeRich Publishing books may be ordered through booksellers or by contacting:

LifeRich Publishing
1663 Liberty Drive
Bloomington, IN 47403
www.liferichpublishing.com
844-686-9607

ISBN: 978-1-4897-3756-4 (sc)
ISBN: 978-1-4897-3755-7 (hc)
ISBN: 978-1-4897-3754-0 (e)

Library of Congress Control Number: 2021915714

Print information available on the last page.

LifeRich Publishing rev. date: 08/19/2021

This book presents information that may challenge what you believe and how you apply that belief. It is so simple yet so challenging that you will need to reread it and take another look at what you believe and how it works in your everyday walk of faith.

There are no magical formulas herein, but there are two facts that may challenge you: who you are may be a startling revelation, and when you go outside yourself looking for God, you go away from God.

Take the challenge. Take another look.

Mary Rose Traylor

Scripture references come from the King James Version (KJV), the New International Version (NIV), and the Eastern Standard Version (ESV).

Throughout this book, I have used the word Ye'shua most often rather than the name Jesus. Various studies have shown that the name Jesus was derived from several translations and is now used throughout most English-speaking regions.

Robert B. Strimple wrote in his book *The Modern Search for the Real Jesus* (1995) that the name Jesus as used by English speakers today is an English adaptation of a German transliteration of a Latin transliteration of a Greek transliteration of an original Hebrew name. According to Strimple, Ye'shua was a common alternative form of the name יְהוֹשֻׁעַ (Yehoshua, Joshua) in later books of the Hebrew Bible and among Jews of the Second Temple period. The name corresponds to the Greek spelling Iesous, from which through the Latin Ieosus comes the English spelling Jesus.

You will find many definitions and explanations as to the spelling and use of the word Jesus as well as Ye'shua. I chose to use Ye'shua.

CONTENTS

WORDS OF WISDOM

It is written that Ye'shua, aka, Jesus spoke and said "That which is born of the flesh is flesh; and that which is born of the Spirit is spirit. Marvel not that I said unto thee, Ye must be born again." (John 4:6–7 KJV)

The apostle Paul, who influenced early Christianity second only to Jesus, said,

Let this mind be in you, which was also in Christ, who thought it not robbery to be equal with God. (Philippians 4:5 KJV).

Be not conformed to this world, rather, be ye transformed by the renewing of your mind. (Romans 12:2b KJV).

Ye'shua said, "You cannot put new wine in old skeins—the fermentation will cause them to burst" (Luke 5:37 KJV).

He that hath ears to hear, let him hear. (Matthew 11:15 KJV)

God told Jeremiah, "I will put My Laws in their minds and write them on their hearts" (Jeremiah 31:33 NIV).

God, the divine spirit, said, "There must be a conversion, a change in mind, before the message of the new world will be planted." Born in sin refers to being born in the atmosphere of the gospel of the kingdom, where the language is insufficient for new-world communication. The man that the world calls Jesus, the Messiah, prophesied about the coming age, but the ground had not been broken.

The apostle Paul wrote, "Forgetting (forget) those things which are past ..." (Philippians 3:13 KJV).

Ye'shua said, "No man who puts his hand to the plough and looks back is not fit for the kingdom" (Luke 9:62 KJV).

Mother Cora Brice of Triumph the Church and Kingdom of God in Christ, Pittsburgh, wrote, "In this mind where Christ does reign ..." Think on the Christ within.

God told me, "Many wolves present themselves in sheep's clothing and say that they come in the name of the Father but come only to steal, kill, and destroy."

FOREWORD

How can you be sure about anything pertaining to eternal life, salvation, and your own conversion? You must look, look again, and then take another look. The looking you need to do to answer the many questions you may have about salvation, life, living, and the purpose for it all must be done with your whole self—your eyes, ears, and heart. What do you see when you look beyond the words that are so loosely spoken that they seem to float in the atmosphere? Look and see, listen to hear, for it is the letter that kills but the Holy Spirit that gives life.

Come let us read and study together. Let us begin to acquire knowledge; the lack of it causes seekers to get lost and the people of God to perish. As you read this book with an open mind and willing spirit, you will have much to look forward to. Seek that you may find and ask that you may receive what you need to gain spiritual understanding.

You were so loved at your conception that you were born free with the memory of purity and perfection. That freedom empowers you to determine your journey. Your freedom and your memory of purity and perfection are rooted in the love of God. It is so intense that it will lead you as you move toward your destiny whatever that may be. As you grow in your freedom and your memory of purity and perfection, you will find that you have the power to call forth whatever you need or desire. You are the master of your destiny.

As you read, the way you see yourself and things around you may begin to look different. You may come to realize that you are special and that your life has a purpose. You are necessary and important. You have been anointed and appointed. You are being readied for victory.

DEDICATION

I dedicate this book to those who identify themselves as seekers of divine truth. My prayer is that what is written herein will strengthen, encourage, uplift, inspire, and empower them.

> You will seek me and find me when you seek me with all your heart. (Jeremiah 29:13 NIV)

> For I know the thoughts that I think toward you saith the Lord; thoughts of peace and not evil, to give you an expected end. (Jeremiah 29:11 KJV)

This book is dedicated to you. I pray that you will be empowered to overcome all disbeliefs, that your tears will subside, your sorrows will turn to joy, and your pain and suffering will be lost. I pray that you find what you are seeking, that what you are asking will be answered, that darkness will turn to light, that mountains will become stepping-stones, and that you will prosper in all do.

Peace, love, and abundant blessings.

IN MEMORY OF

My mother, Mattie Viola Wilson (1998).

My brother, J. Alphonso (Al) Brown (2016).

My granddaughter, De'ja Brittany Green (2014).

7th District Mother of Triumph the Church and Kingdom of God in Christ Mother Geraldine M. Clark (2019)

Mother Geraldine M. Clark (2019).

SPECIAL APPRECIATION TO

My daughter, Rev. Nina LaVonne Wilson.

My son, Joseph Nathan Henderson, PhD.

My companion and friend, Apostle-elect Sylvester F. Steele.

Rev. Dr. Samuel L. Whitlow.

… For their love, prayers, and support.

ABOUT THE BOOK

While reading portions of *Take Another Look*, I heard the author's warm, kind voice regarding religious ideologies and doctrine as she conversed on a subject that is serious and dear to her heart. The read was quite clear and understandable, and it presented in a pleasant conversation that allows readers to adjust their opinions regarding their beliefs in the efficacy of religion.

As you move throughout the pages, you will become absorbed in them before realizing that the author is taking you down a path that subtly leads you on a journey that may question the basis of your faith and the foundation of your beliefs.

It is espoused throughout this inquiry of faith and religious doctrine that man has the power to destroy death. Proverbs 18:21 says, "Death and life are in the power of the tongue." According to the author, this escape from death is accomplished in part via a gift of love, which conquers all. Of special interest is the central thesis that deviates from Western religions, doctrines, and faiths; it is that eternal-life philosophical views are categorized in two broad concepts.

> If you can believe that you will live again after you die, then why is it so difficult to believe that you can live and not die? —M. R. Traylor (Psalm 117:5)

Judaism, Christianity, and Islam are in the majority in Western religions (emulating from the descendants of Shem, a monotheistic belief in the one God, the God of Abraham). In contrast, the views of Buddhism, Hinduism, Taoism, Confucianism, and Shinto are in the majority in

Eastern religions. Typically, Eastern religions are polytheistic meaning that there is more than one God that may be worshipped through different paths.

As it is with most studies in the pursuit of knowledge or understanding, when it comes to religion and politics, the voice is strong on either side of the pendulum; it rarely falls in the middle. As such, the doctrine as explained by the author quite eloquently is based on research and partially on the view of God's existence utilizing a construct—Where he abides and how he abides. Does he abide in you in spirit, dwell in the Son as a human, and/or exist as God the Deity, the Trinity? The author presents a scenario (biblically supported) that aligns with a combination of religious beliefs yet veers into an area that emphasizes self-actualization of the God spirit in oneself.

What do you believe? You are invited to consider a state of existence you may or may not agree with. An understanding of this author's view depends on your experiential (family upbringing or formal church teachings) religious belief, which challenges you to study; 2 Timothy 2:15 (KJV) tells us, "Study to shew thyself approved unto God, a workman that needeth not to be ashamed, rightly dividing the word of truth."

Among the primary concerns of the author in this study is God's love and forgiveness of humanity, which covers a multitude of sins—intentional, unintentional, heinous, trivial, intended or not, etc.—as revealed in one of his compassionate demonstrations of atonement, which epitomizes the bridge to eternal life. One can often find a characterization of how man proposes to share this love outlined indirectly in wedding vows: "Love as symbolized in a ring's promise of no beginning and no end in a life of love, harmony, etc." Love is possible. According to this study, love must be achieved if one hopes to enter a oneness state with God and attain eternal life.

The author outlines the concept of love as the final frontier in understanding the who, what, when, and where of God's existence. Whether you accept the one God who permits death (the end of life) or eternal life, you can appreciate that love is a pivotal point in all your understanding, knowledge, and wisdom. The author purports that love opens the possibilities of considering that there exists one, two, three …

even a dozen ways to understand but not necessarily accept the views not aligned with monotheism.

The author encourages you to not just consider eternal life but also to embrace it by studying, praying, and becoming one with God as a part of your love—agape love, selfless, universal love—for your Creator and others that eventually yields reconciliation.

Overall, this is a great read and a candid view of how one can live eternally apart from the monotheistic view of God in our lives.

—Elder O. C. Rawls, PhD, DTh

INTRODUCTION

> People are destroyed for lack of knowledge; because you have rejected knowledge, I reject you from being a priest to me. (Hosea 4:6 ESV)

> For the wages of sin is death but the gift of God is eternal life through Ye'shua the Christ our Lord. (Romans 6:23 KJV)

Let us see what we can make of these two scriptures. If people are destroyed for lack of knowledge and the wage of sin is death, would it be reasonable to say that lack of knowledge is the sin—the wages that cause death? If lack of knowledge is the sin, would it be reasonable to say that people can destroy death rather than be destroyed by it?

While you are thinking about that, look at another scripture that verifies the power that man must destroy death. Proverbs 18:21 (KJV) states, "Death and life are in the power of the tongue: and they that love it shall eat the fruit thereof." If those who love the power they have over life and death love having that power and appreciate the ability and opportunity to use it, they will feast on the results they will obtain when they use it. Do you understand what it means to speak life and live, speak health, and be delivered from the effects of sickness or diseases that wreak havoc on life?

> Therefore, I say unto you, what things soever ye desire, when ye pray, believe that ye receive them, and ye shall have them. (Mark 11:24 KJV)

It does not require a gigantic amount of faith to use the power in the tongue.

> If you have faith as a mustard seed, you can say to this mulberry tree, Be pulled up by the roots and be planted in the sea,' and it would obey you. (Luke 17:6 NIV)

With just the tiniest bit of faith, even as a beginning believer, you can use your innate power to change your life, your world, and your affairs.

You need faith—belief in what most others consider impossible—to be victorious. However, your faith must be in what has been proven to be true, not what has been devised to capture and deceive you. It will take unadulterated faith to be an overcomer. It will take mustard-seed faith to come out from among those who have conformed to the ways of the world. To live in the ways of the extraordinary God, you will need to believe in your ability to be extraordinary. You can if you believe you can. God is the embodiment of truth in you.

The teachings of certain new-world thinkers whom seekers are learning from focuses on two main ideas: one thought is that there is no separation between God and man, that God dwells in man as his life and breath. The second idea is that the man is the flesh image of God's idea of himself. In this same thought, some believers such as Triumphants, yogis, and Black Hebrews for example recognize Ye'shua as representing the man of flesh dwelling in the land of man. If we take the Genesis account of creation, we must thank the Creator for his pardoning grace. Whenever or however, it happened, man lost the conscious realization of his likeness of God, who created him. Yet the oneness of God in man and man in God was not nor has it ever been disconnected. Praise God for grace and mercy!

When the instructions given to God's created idea of itself were not obeyed, man, created as spirit just like his Creator, was not punished by actual death. Rather, his nakedness was covered with flesh and the ability to think independently of his divine nature. However, man in his pure and holy state yet lives in the flesh. The divine Creator yet speaks to and through the divine nature, the divine consciousness of the God man of flesh. Extraordinary teaching for extraordinary seekers.

This book will inform you that God is still divinely connected to his creation. He dwells in you as the life of the body of flesh and in his consciousness. He is ready at any time to receive you into the glory that is and always has been yours. Man is the glory of God, but the illumination of that glory is buried in the ego, the consciousness of the flesh and blood human.

More about that principle will be taught and better understood when you study as it is admonished in 2 Timothy 2:15 (KJV) and Matthew 5:2 (KJV), which shows that humans must study and be taught: "And he opened his mouth and taught them." The idea of eternal life living in the body is inconceivable by most who have been and are rooted in denominational thoughts and understanding. The promise of God is that man should live and glorify him throughout eternity. However, teachings that those who served would receive their reward in heaven sometime in the unforeseeable future kept alive the idea of another land for man somewhere above the sky. That idea yet lingers in the minds of a majority of religious and denominational members; however, God has promised to lead you through the struggles and limitations of human life into the promise of eternal life to be lived in bodies of flesh that have been transformed into bodies that will live and glorify God.

This book aims to help readers view what they have believed from the beginning until now but from a different point of view. Is it possible that there was more to the sermons you have heard, from Bible study, from others' testimonies, from the songs sung in church? Proverbs 14:12 (KJV) tells us, "There is a way which seems right unto a man, but the end thereof is the ways of death." The scripture does not say that the ways are death; rather, they are the ways of death. That appears to mean that the vibrant, enthusiastic, energetic way of living is not there, which indicates something that is alive with the intelligent, energetic force called God.

This book will not tell you how to eradicate sickness and suffering or how to defeat death, but it will tell you that sickness and suffering can be conquered, and death can be defeated. Sickness and suffering can be conquered because it is not God's will that any should be sick or suffer. Death can be defeated because it is an enemy—and it is to be destroyed.

And I heard a great voice out of heaven saying, Behold, the tabernacle of God is with men, and he will dwell with them, and they shall be his people, and God himself shall be with them, and be their God. And God shall wipe away all tears from their eyes; and there shall be no more death, neither sorrow nor crying, neither shall there be any more pain: for the former things are passed away. (Revelation 21:3–4 KJV)

You have the power to overcome what causes death. Overcoming sickness, suffering, and death is the responsibility of believers everywhere including and especially those in the Black nation, which was first to receive the anointing. Look at what you are exposed to that is responsible for causing you to become victimized by sickness and disease. The world's environment is polluted with negativity, lies, deceit, and falsities. Truth and realness have been lost in the world's lust for ego-pleasing substances. It is necessary for you to overcome those falsities and negativity here in the land of man that lead to the last enemy—death. Hosea 4:6 (KJV) tells us, "My people are destroyed for lack of knowledge." Not knowing that you have the power to defeat the bad circumstances and situations in your life, health, relationships, affairs, and total state of being has the same effect as not having any power.

Whether you know it or not, you have the power to defeat all the debilitating thoughts that lead to a life of suffering and eventually death. You can defeat the negative in your life by not conforming to teachings that lead you down a path to something outside yourself. A transformed life can and will be manifested when you and all believers and seekers realize that the power of life is in all of us. It exists in the uppermost realm of consciousness. That will be revealed when we all become of one accord in our thinking. When we all cease to conform to the limited ways and thinking of this physical world, when we all recognize the Christ dwelling in each of us, when we all recognize that we are spiritual and that all things pertaining to God are spiritual, the heaven we all desire will be revealed.

If you believe that you will live again after you die, why is it so difficult to believe that you can live and not die?

The dead cannot sing praises to the LORD, for they have gone into the silence of the grave. (Psalm 117:15 ESV)

I have written this book so that you can reexamine what you have held onto without questioning its worthiness or truth. Are you steadfast in what you believe, or are you just holding onto what you have heard and followed all your life? Religion is not what will reveal God in his realness or the truth about God and the relationship you should be experiencing with him. Because of the euro-centric religious reign and misinterpretations of sacred writings and spirituality, you may not have been exposed to the truth.

It is my desire to present the teaching as it has been revealed to me about you and God and spiritual matters from a different point of view. Are you willing to consider the possibility of there being something different from what you have been taught and have believed? All it takes to experience a spiritual quickening that will reveal yourself and God from a different perspective is opening your mind and proceed with a mustard seed of faith.

God is the governing force in your life regulating every breath, directing the flow of your bodily fluids, and governing the activity of every organ in your body, yet God is spirit and not human; he exists in a body other than the body called you. God in you is the life of you. It lives and moves as you do, and you are living and moving as the God spirit in a body of flesh. We have been told and led to believe for such a long time that God is something who lives in a place called heaven. It will probably take a long time to change how humankind thinks of and views God. That change may never come, but it is still true that God is in you, and you are in God; you and God are one.

Your culture has shaped everything you say you know about God. Who told you that the Bible was or is the Word of God? Who verified that it was spoken by God through men who may or may not have existed? All the thoughts you have, all you rely on as truth, all you credit to something called God has been shaped by your culture. You were Baptist, Catholic, Methodist, Church of God in Christ, Apostolic, Yorba, Muslim, something else or nothing at all because of what your parents were associated with or something else you were influenced by. Throughout your life, you have been given opportunities and reasons to consider what to believe. Some may have chosen to join a religious organization for any of many reasons. Some may have chosen not to associate with organized religion at all and privately hold onto something they believe in that keeps hope alive for them.

Regardless of what has influenced you, you were born with the spirit of God in you as your life and breath. The life in you was and is eternal. It was a gift you received while you were an idea in the mind of your eventual earthly mother and father, but the spirit of God remained connected to you. Before either of them was shaped and formed by their mothers and fathers, you existed in the "us" who called forth creation. You existed in the mind of the universe. God in you is the life that has and will exist eternally. Life is everlasting.

God has given you a gift that cannot be surpassed—eternal life. The only thing that can limit the eternality of that gift is death. However, dear reader, remember that the power of life and death is in your tongue. Call forth life and live or believe in and speak death; it will be as you desire. Speak life and live. Think life and live.

As a man thinks so is he. (Ezekiel 18:32 KJV)

For I have no pleasure in the death of him that dieth, saith the Lord GOD: wherefore turn yourselves, and live ye.

In Ezekiel 33:11 (KJV), God called those who live ungodly lives to "live, saith the Lord God, I have no pleasure in the death of the wicked; but that the wicked turn from his way and live … for why will ye die?"

God did not give the gift of life so that His people would live for some years and then get sick, suffer, and die.

For the grave cannot praise you. Death cannot sing your praise. Those who go down to the [grave] cannot hope for your faithfulness. (Isaiah 38:18)

People will say, "Ye'shua died so that we can live again with him. It is recorded that Ye'shua said, 'If I go, I will come again and receive you unto myself.'" This says that if he goes, he will come again and receive you, not that he will come again and take you somewhere. In John 17:23 (KJV),

Ye'shua identified the real Trinity that included those who believed and were waiting for the change that would transform their mortal bodies into immortal bodies so that they could live eternally in the land of man with God as the ruler. Ye'shua prayed, "I in them, and thou in me, that they may be made perfect in one" (John 17 KJV).

May you be uplifted, inspired, encouraged, and empowered as you read my triumphant life story and the way God will reveal himself to you in and through what I have written.

MEDITATION OF FAITH

For just a few minutes, make yourself as comfortable as you can. Relax.

Be sure that your environment is comfortable. Relax.

Begin to slow your breath by inhaling deeply.

Be conscious of each breath. Breathe slowly.

Inhale slowly and deeply. Relax.

Feel your breath moving through your body. Relax.

Repeat five or six times and prepare yourself for a journey of faith.

PART I

CHAPTER 1
AT FIRST SIGHT

"I see a new world for me." It is no wonder that a writer could write that with assurance. As you make your journey through the human experience, you encounter many challenges. Sometimes, it seems as if the world is a stumbling-block. Then there are times when it seems as if you have awakened in the middle of an overheated furnace. There are also times when it seems that your tear ducts are stuck in the on position. The hard times are so forceful until it seems as if the good times are rare and premium and have detoured around you. Yet the reality of those times is in the power you have given them by believing they exist. You make them reality by holding onto them.

Do not get dismayed and turn away. Read and see if you can be convinced to take another look at the reality that is yours as stated in Jeremiah 29:11. In that scripture, you are encouraged to hold on, keep the faith, and know that your true reality has already been determined. Your reality is yours to accept or reject. You have held onto something you do not want without seeking another way or something that will bring different results.

Could the writer have been inspired by troubles and dismay to write, "After all these troubles ... I see a new world for me"? Some diseases are so rare that they have not even been named. There are sicknesses that never end—sick bodies, sick minds, sick relationships, sick bank accounts ...

Still, the writer wrote, "After all these troubles over land and sea, I see a new world for me."

Revelation 21:1 (KJV) reads, "I saw a new heaven and a new earth." Do we need to reexamine the world in which we live? Do we need to have different expectations of the people and things we interact with and have influenced our lives? Do we need to clean our glasses? What do we need to do to see the new world that the writer wrote about?

In both those references, the writers must have been forced to look at what they saw in a vision. They must have determined that whatever was going on in their immediate reality would pass and a new opportunity would come out of what they were seeing. Was it just an illusion? Was something going on in the reality that both writers were experiencing—perhaps some type of mental stress that made them disillusioned?

The apostle Paul admonished the early Roman Christians to "be transformed by the renewing of their minds." The vision and revelation both writers experienced could have been the beginning of a transformation of their minds. They saw something beyond their physical reality. I wonder if it was something we should be looking for.

The world in which we live is full of illusions, lost hope, and broken dreams that seem to crowd out what good there is in our world. We see the fragments of such all around, yet if we would look from a different point of view, if we would take a different perspective, might it be possible to see the world differently? By we, I refer to those the scripture refers to as having "ears [that] are dull of hearing, and ... eyes [that are open but do not see]." These are those who are born of the Spirit and seek to rise to a higher level of divine wisdom and understanding. They are seeking to obtain a more spiritual persuasion.

We are advised to seriously consider whether we are ready to see a new world, whether we are ready to be transformed by renewed minds. Are we ready to change our point of view? Are we ready to see a new world in a valley, on a mountain, at the seashore, on a beach, or on a roof? Are we ready to let go of what we claim is our present reality? Are we ready to be transformed so we can walk and not grow weary or run and not faint? Are we ready to make our circumstances and situations conform to our desires?

Are we ready to assume our God-given power?

The greatest, most powerful principle that can lead to a highly spiritual living experience says that God's will is that all should live an abundant life. Accordingly, we all can if we look at all our experiences of living different from what is appearing as our present reality. We cannot allow what we see when we look at the circumstances and situations of our physical humanness to block our spiritual views.

Because your human makeup is limited to what you can see, hear, taste, touch, and feel physically, your interpretations of them is limited to what I call surface understanding. You can see the reality of a new world rich and free with a surface understanding from a different point of view. To see that new world written and sung about, view and interpret your experiences through your mind's eye, there must be something different from the limited ability of the physical that eyes cannot see. The physical eyes can behold only what is created to be viewed in the physical by the physical. What is spiritual is of the spirit.

> That which is born of the flesh is flesh, and that which is
> born of the Spirit is spirit. (John 3:6 ESV)

Some have embraced the concept of believing or even knowing that to live eternally in the body we now live in is possible and even probable. (Read 1 Corinthians 15:51.) From the very beginning, humanity was to live as the Creator lived—from everlasting to everlasting—as spiritual beings. Humanity was to have the power to create as the Creator did.

> And the Lord God said, Behold, the man is become as one
> of us, to know good and evil: and now, lest he put forth
> his hand, and take also of the tree of life, and eat, and live
> forever. (Genesis 3:22 KJV)

Because of the advanced knowledge man discovered, he became aware of his ability to make decisions independent of his Creator. His awareness made him just like his Creator; however, he did not have the wisdom necessary to use this knowledge. This creature was created to possess the knowledge, but it was to develop over time as the man grew into his

I-deity, his identity. The creative experience had brought forth itself, its own image, in another form after its likeness.

There it was—the master Creator pregnant with the idea of another image exactly like himself. What an idea! "[At man's awakening he] shall know that I am in my Father, and ye in me, and I in you" (John 14:20 KJV). That means, my sisters and brothers, that we are each one in the oneness of God the Father, Son, and Holy Spirit.

As the idea of reproduction began to come forth, it was obvious that love was the determining factor. Despite what did or did not exist and despite the environmental circumstances, situations, and conditions, the idea of life was being pushed into existence by the power of divine love. It did not matter that it was dark. Man's understanding had not yet developed; no other idea had penetrated the consciousness or mind, where life was forming. It did not matter that water, which metaphysically means unexpressed possibilities, was lurking in the darkness (where there was no understanding) still in seed form and waiting for somewhere to take root. The Creator was able to see himself in the image of himself. It was a beautiful, masterful, and powerful image of himself. Thus, a love affair began—love and life that were pure and perfect. The soul of life was and still is love, and the soul of love was and still is life.

CHAPTER 2
AS IT WAS

The energizing, driving force of life is love. Love by itself cannot be viewed as the pure energy it is. Rather, love manifests itself by the way life is lived physically. This could be a once-upon-a-time story; however, it was what it was, and it was more than one could imagine. Life had brought forth the idea of itself and it was love at first sight. The union of love and life was intense, and the process of reproduction continued.

The purity of love was so bright that life could not stand the glow. Therefore, love began to make a covering for itself—flesh—and it developed into another being composed of love and life. It became known as the third part of the union—man. The second trinity was life, love, and man. It began to reproduce as a vessel containing the spiritual characteristics of the original creative energy and its own creative powers. Remember, it was created with the same abilities of its Creator. Each reproduction however became more and more dominant in the likeness of the original Creator. What an awesome creature you are!

Through the process of time, creation remained as it had been created to be. It grew more independent and further away from what it was created to do—serve and nurture all life forms created by divine energy. All of what the Creator is was embedded in the seed of life that was to reproduce itself and bring forth pure, holy, God images, God ideas. As it was in the beginning, it is now and ever shall be. Hallelujah! The original idea of life is still alive, which is why life is eternal.

We all know or have heard some versions of the creation story as well as the story of reproduction. The way you have received and interpreted that story determines how you feel about and accept the idea of life eternal. The apostle Paul admonished the Roman Christians to "be not conformed to 'this' world, but to be transformed by the renewing of [their] mind(s)" (Romans 12:2 KJV). To understand the idea of living forever in these bodies, you must understand what it means to be transformed. You must seek divine understanding of God's intention for the life of his creation. Ask yourself, did God create man in his divine image to live for a specific number of years only, or did he create man to live as he lived? Ezekiel 16:6 (KJV) reads,

> And when I passed by you and saw you struggling in your own blood, I said to you in your blood, "Live!" Yes, I said to you in your blood, "Live!"

This scripture was a specific prophecy of Ezekiel to Jerusalem, but the same holds true for man of all times. Life is not in the scriptures or in the blood of the human body (there must be a spiritual transformation); the assurance of eternal life is in the promise of life God—divine energy—has given. With all our getting, we must get an understanding.

According to the scripture, man's lack of understanding of God and himself led him to behave in an adverse manner and then hide because of what ensued. The curse was for a hard life and death. However, the curse of death and the Mosaic law (i.e., "an eye for an eye") were fulfilled and justified.

> Think not that I am come to destroy the law, or the prophets: I am not come to destroy, but to fulfill. (Matthew 5:17 KJV)

> And there shall be no more curse. (Revelation 22:3 KJV)

The energetic force we identify as God is eternal. Therefore, to be in the image of God, the created is, must be, can only be eternal just as he is.

Living is the physical activity done with the spiritual gift of life. Your living experiences are manifestations of your world, and your affairs reflect your consciousness, where your thoughts are processed. Your thoughts are of the spirit but may not be interpreted at the spiritual level of consciousness. What enters the conscious mind comes from the super- or subconscious levels.

The subconscious does not analyze, reason, judge, criticize, determine, or do anything except present what is stored in it. It projects all its images to the conscious mind, where all thoughts are processed. The process is done through analyzing, reasoning, judging, and criticizing determinations and opinions formed and acted upon. The conscious mind does not realize that it is a threshing floor. What appears in the conscious mind will be processed and stored in the subconscious.

Thoughts and ideas that enter the conscious mind from the superconscious are divine. The superconscious mind does not analyze, reason, judge, criticize, determine, or scrutinize what passes through it because it comes directly from the universal consciousness or divine energy—God. The revelations or prophecies that come from the superconscious mind will elevate the conscious mind and increase its knowledge, wisdom, and understanding of whatever the revelation or prophecy references. The answers to prayers come through the superconscious mind. All divine ideas, all communication from God to man, originate in the superconscious mind, an umbilical cord that keeps the created connected to the Creator as it was, always has been, and always will be.

When God Speaks

God speaks to man through the superconscious. You must know the voice of God before you can respond to it on the conscious level. His voice is the spoken word. The spirit of God has never stopped speaking to the consciousness of man. In the silence, God still speaks. The winds have carried the voice of God to his people in all directions. His voice can be heard in thunder, birdsong, the buzzing of bees, and in the gurgling of streams.

For too long, man has allowed his mind to be cluttered with noise that keeps the voice of God muffled. Noisy distractions distort the voice of God so that it cannot be heard. Therefore, there can be no understanding, and it may appear that God has stopped talking. When Moses went up the mountain for the Ten Commandments, the Israelites despaired because he was gone for so long. God was speaking, but they did not hear him. He was delivering his plan for his people to Moses.

Sometimes, you may be too quick to give in to distractions that dull hearing and diminish faith. The detachment between our minds and God's voice has made us unable to fully understand our role as beings endowed with divine power. We have suffered as those who have no hope. We feel helpless and alone. Failing to hear God's voice and using the power to overcome our bad circumstances is denying God's plan for us.

> He that believeth on me, the works that I do shall he do also; and greater works than these shall he do. (John 14:12 KJV)

As it was, so it is. All is not forlorn. Even if you do not always hear God's voice, he always hears yours. He is always on call and will always take your call. His line is never busy, and he will never put you on hold or block you from his contact list. All you need to do is start thinking as one church mother, Mother Cora Brice, wrote, "What you want the Lord to do, get it in your mind and keep it in your mind all the time." Job 22:28 (KJV) says, "Thou shall decree a thing and it shall be established unto thee."

If you want to hear the voice of God, desire that. The words in the chorus of a song revealed to and written by me speaks to what I am saying.

> God sees me when I fall, He hears me when I call.
> He speaks to my heart and my soul rejoices
> When I am down and broken, there is no one around,
> God speaks in my soul, and it makes me whole.
> Teach me to listen for your voice, even in the distractive noise all around me.
> Even in my own mind, let your voice resound louder than it all.

Know Yourself

You have been created in the image of the Creator. You are one with the Trinity.

> And God said, Let us make man in our image, after our likeness. (Genesis 1:26 KJV)

> ... that all of them may be one, as You, Father, are in Me, and I am in You. May they also be in Us. I have given them the glory You gave Me, so that they may be one as We are one—I in them and You in Me. (John 17:21–23 KJV)

As you come into a greater awareness and understanding of yourself and God, you are challenged to investigate further your body of flesh and blood. You are challenged to accept that your body is the temple in which God dwells. In you this holy God speaks, and his voice is resounding with every beat of your heart just as it did when it was spoken, "Let there be ..." You are so much more than you have imagined. The distractions of the physical world do not want you to be more than they are. They do not want you to be transformed by renewing your mind.

If you are transformed and do not conform, the physical body will not be the center of attention. Your attention will be geared toward developing your spiritual self while living in your body. Developing your spiritual self will enable you to utilize the power you have to defeat those distractions.

Never allow your mind to be so cluttered with outside noise that you cannot hear God's voice, which is your voice speaking from your God-self. It will guide you to the transformation you need to make. It is a mystery that will come with heightened understanding. With all your getting, get understanding. (See Proverbs 4:7.)

The Word of God can be read in various publications, but the Word that comes to us should not be seen or heard as only words we read or hear. The Word of God is good for inspiration, encouragement, and empowerment. It is good for validation, doctrine, and instructions on how to live. Listening to and reading inspired words when you need to hear them can heighten your awareness of who you are and your connection with God. You should take time, be still, and hear God speaking to you, in you, through you, or through any other medium he chooses to use.

Your heart and lungs keep you alive. The real Word of God is the life of you. You are the living Word of God. By the spoken Word, you were brought forth, pressed out of the Allness of the divine spirit, born of his holiness. By the Word of God, you were given authority and dominion over all the works of your creation. By the Word, you were chosen to be the living son spirit of God.

> I have given you power to become sons of God. (John 1:12 KJV)

As it was, is, and ever shall be.

CHAPTER 3
A NEW POINT OF VIEW

There is a living spirit in the universe—the spirit of triumph. By triumph, I am referring to the spirit that empowers you to live on a higher level of consciousness. It lives in you and all humankind. It is in us to make us aware of the word of truth, which is power in us.

You have been overpowered with religious dogma. You have been expected to accept it without question. How can you be expected to grow into the fullness of your spirituality if you cannot question what you may not understand? Unless you have been taught that you are one with God and are in God as God is in you, you have been denied the truth of your existence.

The basis of knowing who you are in spirit is to know that the kingdom of God is established in the spirit of God, which dwells in you. Therefore, what God is, where God is, there is triumph—power. What an amazing awareness to know that you have the power to see peace where there is confusion, to see truth beyond religious dogma, lies, and half- truths, to see your world without sickness or disease. The power of God in you empowers you to see beyond the limitations of poverty; you have the power to see prosperity at every level, and the spirit of triumph in you empowers you to see beyond death and see life transformed from mortality to immortality. Victory is yours!

The spirit of triumph is empowered with principles and doctrines. It is a way of life that when adhered to will show you how to live so that the new world will always be in view because your thinking will have been changed. Your new way of thinking will transform you. Your consciousness will be infused with something new to focus on. As your thoughts change, your life will change; as a man thinks, so is he. As your mind is renewed, your life will change. The spirit of triumph in you will quicken your mortal mind and cause your eyes to see as they have never seen before. They will see beyond the ordinary to the extraordinary. You will see as others cannot. Your sight will come from a transformed mind. You will see God in all his glory in everything, everywhere, all the time.

If the spirit of triumph is your way of life, your mind will be quickened with the awareness of the living experiences of today. It will guide you into letting go of the practices and principles of former times. Former things are passed away—"But this one thing I do, forgetting those things which are behind." A new world filled with new ideas and a new vision has been given to those who are seeking it. "Behold, I make all things new" (Revelation 21:1 KJV); "I create new heavens and a new earth" (Isaiah 65:17 KJV).

Bishop Elias Dempsey Smith, founder of Triumph the Righteous Church, wrote of a revelation he had in *Triumph—What We Believe and Teach.*

> And he carried me away in the spirit to a great and high mountain and showed me that great city, the holy Jerusalem, descending out of heaven from God. The high mountain is the righteous government of Christ, and Jerusalem is the church. The people are called up into the triumphant life of Christ, which is the eternal life of both soul and body, the overcoming life. "He that hath an ear, let him hear what the Spirit sayeth."

Some believe that there is a place somewhere in the sky, beyond the clouds, another world where God dwells, but Bishop Smith's vision says that God dwells in man. While others believe that all will die and go to heaven to live with God, according to the revelation given to Bishop Smith, we shall live with God here on earth, which will have been glorified, in transformed bodies.

As your consciousness rises, you will be transformed. The more your consciousness rises, the better you will understand your oneness with the spirit of God and the more your appearance will change. As it was with Ye'shua after the resurrection, so it will be with you after your spiritual resurrection. Read about the resurrection of Ye'shua in Luke 24:13–32 and John 20:11–18. When your consciousness rises, when your understanding of the Word of God comes alive in you, those you previously walked and fellowshipped with will not know you. You will not talk, walk, look, or act the way you did before your resurrection. As you continue to study and ask for understanding, you will understand the Word that says, "Be ye transformed by the renewing of your mind" (Romans 12:1–2).

Your body and soul will live with the manifested spirit of God eternally on earth. You may not believe that now, but I encourage you to read, study, meditate, and pray for an understanding of what this means. Many are called ... and since you are reading this, it may be an indication that you are among those chosen and called to this overcoming way of believing and living.

The key is in being transformed to believe that you are God as Andersen wrote in *Three Magic Words* (1954). God lives eternally, and so can you. If you die, it will be because you do not know how to live. If your mind does not grow, it will die, and you will not be counted among those who are alive. It will then be asked of your dead mind, soul, and consciousness, "Why seek you the living among the dead?" You shall know the truth.

The prophecies were fulfilled and passed on through the messianic age, through the gospel of the kingdom era where Ye'shua reigned. It has passed through the Holy Spirit age, the apostolic age, and the Christian era. The prophecies came to pass, and they will when they have fulfilled their purpose including the laws of the Old Testament age.

We are entering the age of revelations, yet fragments of the gospel of the kingdom era linger because people are holding onto the memory of the promises of that era. Since thoughts become things, their thoughts have produced things that linger. The ideas of a heaven in or beyond the sky, the man named Jesus returning to take them somewhere, the idea of Jesus coming to heal their wounds and erase their diseases or otherwise change their circumstances are the kinds of thoughts that keep those believers bound to old ideas. Undesirable conditions linger because people are still holding onto these thoughts in their minds. It is virtually impossible for a new world to come into manifestation if the images of the past linger in our minds. Paul wrote to those in Philippi,

> Brethren, I count not myself to have apprehended: but this one thing I do, forgetting those things which are behind, and reaching forth unto those things which are before, I press toward [forward]. (Philippians 3:13–14a KJV)

There is no way to go forward while looking and living in the past. According to Mark 16:15–17 (KJV),

> Go ye into all the world and preach the gospel to every creature He that believeth and is baptized [immersed in the Word] shall be saved; but he that believeth not shall be damned. And these signs shall follow them that believe; In my name shall they cast out devils; they shall speak with new tongues; They shall take up serpents; and if they drink any deadly thing, it shall not hurt them; they shall lay hands on the sick, and they shall recover.

This admonishment is a clear indication that commissioned believers are to live beyond the time of Ye'shua. Believers are to move forward establishing a world where men will live in the Christ consciousness (the conscious thought that it is not robbery to be equal with God), where the mind of Christ reigns and the peace of God covers the earth.

The time of Ye'shua has been fulfilled. This is a new day, a new dispensation. This is the day when the teachings and examples of Ye'shua must be expanded. It must be proven and determined that the Word of God is eternal. Truth is eternal. Ye'shua gave the power to his followers, and from then until now, the power has been established with anointed and appointed believers. All have the power to work the work of the anointing upon them. Some have the power to be apostles, and some prophets, and some evangelists, and some pastors and teachers. for the perfecting of the saints, for the work of the ministry, for the edifying of the body of Christ. (Ephesians 4:11–12 KJV)

The world is now in a transitory period; men are living in the darkness of their carnal minds. The time of carnality—this era when ignorance is causing a falling away like dry leaves from trees—is ending. Truth is springing forth like young seedlings after a long winter. The earth—the carnality—of man is being ridded of the limited information of the past and the good news message of the new season is the declaration of the reality of eternal life in the body. As it is written in Revelation 21:4, the reality is that man can live this side of death! You, like David in Psalm 118:17–18 (ESV), can declare, "I shall not die, but live, and declare the works of the Lord. The LORD ... hath not given me over unto death."

Death is the only enemy that threatens eternal life.

The revelation of triumph that came to Apostle Smith in 1897 and the message the spirit of triumph proclaims today is what should motivate you to keep moving forward. Regardless of what others are saying in their songs, sermons, testimonies, and prayers, triumphant believers and seekers should keep reaching for the new revelation—Man can live and not die.

According to scripture, Ye'shua was telling a story of a guest at a wedding who was not dressed in a traditional wedding garment. When asked why that was, the host replied, "Many are called, but only a few are chosen." Thus, it is with the message in Apostle Smith's revelation and in the teachings of triumph. Both have a message for the new age. Many will hear the message but will not take it to heart. According to Smith, when he shared his revelation with other ministers, some said that the message was good but that the people would not believe it. Others said that his message was good but was too soon, that people would not receive it. Someone once told me that people in denominational churches would turn a deaf ear to the message of eternal life living in the body. She said that they would not even accept the revelation that God is not a being out there or up there somewhere. I know that God is the energetic force we call life dwelling in all living beings. In man, it is the breath of life. It saturates every fiber of the physical body giving it life. It filters through every organ, every nerve, and every cell giving directions for them all to function as they were created to function. Nothing lives without the force we call God dwelling in it. When you focus your attention on anything outside yourself, you are going away from the God you are praying to. God is all around you, and He is greater in you than anywhere else. Ye'shua said in John 14:20 (KJV), "At that day ye shall know that I am in my Father and ye in me, and I in you." If you are ready for the message for this new day, this new era, hear what the spirit is saying.

We know now that it is not too soon for the message. Others are preaching it, teaching it, testifying to it, singing it, and discussing it in everyday conversations—"Man can live and not die." Today, we believe that "soon there will be no hearse wheels rolling" (Mother Cora Brice).

CHAPTER 4
THE DAY OF REVELATION

The age of revelation, like the messianic age, has come to enlighten the chosen, those set apart for the dawning of the day of revelation, the day of victorious deliverance, the day when man hears and becomes fully aware of and in control of the power he has over his life. Luke 10:19 (ESV) says, "Behold, I have given you authority to tread on serpents and scorpions, and over all the power of the enemy, and nothing shall hurt you."

Who are those set aside for the coming age of revelation? You are! If you have opened your mind to accept the reality of the indwelling God spirit, if you have attuned your ear to hear the revealed Word and discern it from the noisy pestilence, you are among those chosen to behold the dawning of the day of revelation, the moment you realize that life is yours to live from everlasting to everlasting.

You can live eternally in your body—which will be redeemed and changed from mortal to immortal ("Behold, I show you a mystery, not all shall sleep," 1 Corinthians 15:51 KJV)—and you have the spiritual ability to triumph over the very idea of not living in your body in this land of man. When you focus on the fact that you have the power to overcome whatever confronts you, you will no longer give power and energy to anything outside yourself that threatens the life in you.

You can love your conditions and circumstances into what you want them to be, or you can speak the Word—There is power of life and of death in the tongue—and watch the universe respond. If anything in your life needs to be brought under subjection to the power you have, now might be a good time to try it and see if the spirit in you will connect with the spirit of the universe and bring about a change. Anything that is not your friend is your enemy, and according to Luke as stated above, you have power over your enemies. Hallelujah, amen!

The era of revelation is a time when the quickening spirit makes known the truth about God in man and about life and death. The day and time will come when the meaning of the oneness of God and man will be revealed. Ye'shua taught, "I am in the Father, and you are in Me, and I am in you." You are one in the oneness of the Trinity—God, Son, and Holy Spirit. If you believe, you can do works even greater than those Ye'shua did. As a man, the Son did the work of God on earth to teach all they were capable of doing and becoming. The Holy Spirit is the activity of the Father working in and on behalf of the total man, and it is carrying on the work begun by Ye'shua.

The era of revelation is the era when false prophets, liars, deceivers, and wolves in sheep's clothing are exposed. Believers and seekers who have not conformed to this world, who have been waiting for the manifestation of Jeramiah 29:11, will prosper in this era. The era of revelation brings a higher message directly from God to those who desire a higher anointing. God has a message for those who choose to be delivered from the bonds of complacency. Ye'shua called men to go with him. Those men were exposed to a way of life that was much different from the way they were living. They were taught and shown things that were difficult for them to understand or believe. They were taught and exposed to things that they thought were impossible in preparation for the life they would live. They were being prepared for the work they would do when they were commissioned to go into the world and do as Ye'shua had taught them.

Ye'shua informed all humans of their innate power. He came to teach humanity how to live. He healed the sick, and he raised the dead. Symbolically, raising the dead had a dual message—bodies can die, spirit cannot die, spirit is the life of the body. Lazarus had been dead for four days, but he came forth when he was called. Life in man is eternally connected to the spirit of God, which is the breath of life in man. When you realize your connection with the spirit of God in you, when you recognize the power you have because of that spirit, you can call forth life into dying joy, dying peace, dying confidence, dying self-esteem, and dying health conditions. Your circumstances and situations can be resurrected!

The spirit of God in you is your power source activated by the Holy Spirit that empowers you to tell your lame circumstances to get up and walk. You can tell your blind situations to go wash and open their eyes and see. You can tell your deaf conditions to hear what the spirit is saying. You can cast your doubts and fears into a lake of forgetfulness.

Dear reader, you have the power to be victorious in all you do. Sickness, suffering, death, and dying are not your divine inheritance. You may have come forth from the seed of your earthly dad and through the womb of your mother, but your true DNA is of God. Claim your identity and inheritance and live them. Do not conform to anything less than your divine right. Rise into the newness of life. The Holy Spirit can elevate you to the height of your transformed consciousness. Reach out to it, desire a change of mind to a nonconformed mind, a new way of seeing, thinking, being, living, knowing, and you will be baptized and changed by the quickening of the Holy Spirit. The work you begin will be completed by the spirit of God in you. It happened before during the time of Yeshua's teaching, it happened during the ministries of the apostles, and it is happening today.

The Holy Spirit came during the messianic age as a dove at the symbolic baptizing of Ye'shua (Spong 2002). It remained with Ye'shua during his human experience. When Ye'shua transitioned, the Holy Spirit became active in the mind of man to remind him of what he had been admonished to do, how he had been admonished to live, and the work he had been admonished to continue.

> The comforter [Holy Spirit] will come and it will bring to
> your remembrance all things whatsoever I [Ye'shua] have
> commanded you. (John 14:26 KJV)

19

The Holy Spirit makes Yeshua's teachings as alive today as they were during his time. It continues to minister to and teach us on a higher level. Since we are in the Son and the Son is in us, a victorious life is ours. We have the right to walk the path of righteousness, the way of triumph. I call it that because it was in a congregation identified as Triumpians that I began to see the possibility of what I had only imagined most of my life. The teachings of Triumph have made available to you the freedom to discover the reality of God in you and you in God and what that means as you strive to live as a spiritual being in this human world. This path of righteousness is for those who choose to conquer all their bonds, fears, doubts, and limitations including sickness, suffering, and even death.

> Yea, tho I walk through the valley of the shadow(s) ... I will fear nothing for thy spirit is with me. (Psalm 23:4 KJV)

> Old things are passed away. And God (in you) shall wipe away all tears from [your] eyes, and there shall be no more death, neither sorrow, nor crying, neither shall there be any more pain; for the former things are passed away. (Revelation 21:4 KJV)

Just as the teachings of the prophets and Ye'shua and other enlightened messengers were meant to awaken those of that era who were seeking to understand the message of Ye'shua, it is likewise today. The revelation and writings of books such as this one is for those of this day who have not conformed to this world, who have been standing solid on the foundation of new prophecies. These words come from God through the Holy Spirit onto the pages of books such as this one. This information has come to speak truth and lead you, the readers, down the path of righteousness. It can be yours if you surrender to the wisdom and guidance of the Holy Spirit.

Those who embrace these truths today are awakened and enlightened. Now, however, you can choose to go forward to a greater revelation and a deeper truth. You have been injected with the power of Christ, and the awareness of your immortality is in you waiting for your acknowledgment and acceptance!

Immortality

Immortality is a reality that has not yet penetrated the mind of man. Death has been defined as a part of life. Now that is an oxymoron, because death is an enemy that must and will be destroyed (1 Corinthians 15:26). Isaiah 25:8 reads, "Oh death where is thy sting?" It must be destroyed, and you have power over your enemies. Death will not be destroyed by a battle fought in the sky but in the minds of true believers who identify with the scriptures, other revealed writing, and teachings including the way of life and teachings of Triumph. When we all get together in our thinking, when we all get the new world in our view, when we all see God as it is—spirit and man being one—mortality will give way to immortality and life will be as it has been from everlasting to everlasting in elevated consciousness and redeemed bodies transformed by the thoughts of renewed minds.

A search on the internet of the word *immortality* said that it was

> eternal life, being exempt from death, unending existence. Some modern species may possess biological immortality. Certain scientists, futurists, and philosophers have theorized about the immortality of the human body, with some suggesting that human immortality may be achievable in the first few decades of the 21st century. (en. wikipedia.org/wiki/Immortality)

That definition could mean that bodies of flesh and blood will be changed to be immune to the limitations of the flesh. Paul said in 2 Corinthians 5:1 (KJV),

> If this earthly house [body of flesh] of this tabernacle [human consciousness] should be dissolved, we have a building of God, a house [a redeemed body] not made with hands, eternal in the heavens [spiritual consciousness].

God is spirit. Everything pertaining to God is spiritual. Therefore, the heaven we think about is not the place we have heard about. It is not made of substance and cannot be likened to the sun, moon, planets, stars, or clouds. It is a spiritual concept housed in the consciousness of the universe

21

and ultimately in the highest realm of the mind of man, his superconscious. You may have heard that our bodies were the temple of God, but it is not the physical body—flesh and blood—It is the superconscious, where things of the spirit dwell. It is that place in you no carnal thoughts can enter. It is that place in the mind of the carnal man where there are no doubts and fears that limit the power of man, that limit your power to be victorious in the carnal world. To know this and to recognize it as a divine truth opens the mind's eye so that you shall see God as he is. You shall see God, the I Am who is the individual expression of God, which is the I Am—your true self.

From the spiritual point of view, to see a new world, you must allow the awakening, empowering spirit of that new world to project you into that world. You must allow it to make you aware of the power of deliverance that will deliver you from the limitations of the conscious mind, which limits your ability to see things of the spirit without trying to reduce them to human understanding. You must allow the I Am spirit to nourish you with the messianic truth. It must transform your human understanding to be subjected to the Christ wisdom and the bread and wine of the new world. "Trust in the Lord with all your heart and lean not on your own understanding" (Proverbs 3:5 KJV).

The spirit of triumph, a transformed way of life, a life of divine revelation, of Christ wisdom, is for all humankind, but only a few people will choose the way of the spirit, the way of Christ. The last shall be first. Yes, all are invited, but not all will accept the invitation to come to where the table is spread with the new bread of life.

You may be wondering how you can renew your mind so that you become transformed. I wrote earlier about those who hold onto the ways of the world of the flesh. While you cannot live in this world without being concerned with its issues, you must not become consumed with those issues because they will soon pass away and reappear in a different manner. Christian believers look forward to something in the physical world being the power that will transform them. Most believers and nonbelievers prepare to die and go through the grave to be with God and Jesus. However, the power to renew your mind and be transformed is in you. You do not have to go anywhere to be transformed or to be with the Lord. When you change the way you think, a transformation will begin that will redeem the earth—your life, your world, and all that concerns you—of all ungodly thinking. Your behaving will be changed from the carnal to the spiritual. All overcomers, those who are transformed by way of renewed thinking, will live in the new earth, the one John saw coming down from God as recorded in Revelation 21:1–3 (KJV).

> Then I saw a new heaven and a new earth, for the first heaven and the first earth had passed away and there was no longer any sea. I saw the Holy City, the new Jerusalem, coming down out of heaven from God, prepared as bride dressed for her husband. And I heard a loud voice from the throne saying, 'Now the dwelling of God is with men, and he will live with them. They will be his people and he will be their God.

Life is eternal, and it will live on either side of the great divide.

> Behold I tell you a mystery, we shall not all sleep, but we all will be changed. (1 Corinthians 15:51 ESV)

As transformed believers, we are striving to be among those who will not sleep but will be changed. We know that if we remain bound to the ways of carnal thinking, we will live and sleep the sleep of the carnal minded changed but through the process of death. Ezekiel 37 tells us how dry bones were reconnected, covered with new flesh, given a new heart, and brought to life by the breath of God. We will be reconnected to the spirit of life in a way that will spark new life in our carnal bodies. That breath of life will be disconnected from mortality and reconnected to immortality so that we may live on this earth in transformed and gloried bodies.

While we are yet bound to one another by the invisible cord of the breath of life, some have never experienced the quickening power of God, the spirit of life, the breath in us all that makes us one body, one mind, and one life. By the Spirit, the breath of God, all can be changed from mortal to immortal, but all will not experience the change. Whereas all can be changed, all will not allow the change to take place in them, for first, our minds must be changed. The way we visualize the world around us and what our belief systems focus on will empower us to believe that nothing—not even the power of death—will have any effect on all who embrace that quickening spirit.

Mother Cora Brice did not make the change from mortal to immortality in her body, but I believe she saw the coming change when she wrote this.

> Just beyond the veil of darkness there is a form of creative laws, where the force of death has vanished, with the sin (ignorance) that brought its cause, Now the Gentile world has ended with its strength of carnal minds, and the peace of God's salvation keeps me happy all the time ... Soon there will be no hearse wheels rolling, and no funeral bells shall ring, and there will be no carnal minded preachers lying on our Savior and King, For all the people of God shall know them, from the infant to the sire, And we all shall possess healthy bodies, and never more be sick or die ...

> Blessed Triumph ever lead me from this old world dark and wide, Blessed Triumph ever lead me to that new world filled with smiles, Now I see the glorious advent of a new world rich and free, It is mine to have forever, and there I'll spend eternity.

God expressing as man has dominion over all living things in, on, above, and below earth. As the expression of himself as man, he maintains mastery over things that empower man to achieve spiritual bliss. Man has that same power, but he also has mastery over poisons, infections, sickness, distress, and all else that keeps the human from living spiritually happy and healthy.

Dr. Daniel H. Harris, a former chief apostle in Triumph the Church and Kingdom of God in Christ, did not experience the synchronization of the spirit and his physical body, but testimonies were given of his having had a glimpse of what it would be like to live in the spiritual realm. He envisioned the coming new world while he was on a forty-day sabbatical. He had heard about and taught the mystery of God and human living in the same body at the same time, but he was seeking a deeper understanding of that mystery. He knew that there was more to life than what appeared from a human perspective. He also believed deeply in the teachings of everlasting life living in the body, and he sincerely wanted to manifest that belief.

During his sabbatical, he had a vision that showed that man being changed from mortal to immortal without physical death was a reality. It had such an effect on him that he shared his vision with a new testimony that revealed his vision. He testified of having a new world in his view. It so impressed him that he said that from that moment on, that vision would be his new reality. Though he did not obtain the life he saw in his vision, it was real enough to become his new reality. The promise of eternal life of the total man—body, soul, and spirit—is real.

Other writers have written about new ways of thinking about life and living. One writer wrote about living the infinite way, another writer wrote about the idea of everlasting life being a reality, and another wrote about this thing called life. All those writers have seen life from a different perspective. They have seen it from a mountaintop, a view that has overcome the limitations of human conception. They too have seen as John the revelator saw. They have seen what has been revealed as living in the oneness of God.

Today, God is communicating with man on a deeper level. Man is not only seeking for a more expansive understanding of the revelation given to people like Apostle Smith; he is also seeking to know God's plan for the church today. Individually, we have not escaped the turmoil of human life and mortal living; the same hurts, ills, disappointments, sicknesses, and sufferings plague us all. However, we hold to the prophecy in Revelation 21:4–5 KJV: "There will be no more death or mourning or crying or pain, for the old order of things has passed away."

These things, conditions, and circumstances have no place in the world God created for you or the life he desires you to live. His will for you is that you live a happy and healthy life and that you prosper in all your ways. Nothing has power over the will of God. However, since the will of God is free will, you are free to accept or reject it.

Isaiah 54:17 KJV reads, "No weapon formed (seen or unseen, physical, mental, spiritual) against you shall prosper." Every tongue that speaks against you in judgment shall be condemned by you. Stay in the will of God and live by his promises.

PART II
"BEHOLD I SHOW YOU A MYSTERY"

When I mention Christian believers, I am referring to believers who are gospel of the kingdom believers. They are water-baptized believers who will not go beyond the third human world, the world of water and blood, but will receive the fulfillment of the promise made to them—Jesus's death forgave, justified, and redeemed them so that they could live forever after death in the spirit realm with the spirit of the redeemer. Paul wrote in 2 Corinthians 5:1, "For we know that if our earthly house of this tabernacle [were] dissolved, we have a building of God, [a] house not made with hands, eternal in the heaven."

Paul also wrote in 2 Corinthians 5:8, "We are confident, I say, and willing rather to be absent from the body, and to be present with the Lord."

God knows the plan he has for you that will prosper you. He declared that he had plans to give you hope and a future (Jeremiah 29:11).

Triumphant Believers differ from Christian Believers in what they believe in several ways. First, they are referred to as Triumphants because they believe that they will triumph over physical sickness, diseases, all manner of suffering, and even death. They have chosen to follow the revelation of the late Apostle Elias Dempsey Smith, the founder of Triumph the Righteous Church, later to be incorporated as Triumph The Church and Kingdom of God In Christ. They believe that the Holy Ghost leads them to the incarnated Christ consciousness, which is the wisdom and power of God in man. Triumpians further believe that the Paraclete (which is the Holy Ghost) awakens in them the spirit of the new world that John the Revelator saw coming down from God. They also believe that the awakening will deliver their flesh body from the power of death and ransom from the grave and that they will receive the gift of God which is eternal life. They also believe that the gift of eternal life is to be lived in a redeemed and glorified body. (Adapted from the Creed of Triumph the Church and Kingdom of God in Christ, 1982 Constitution).

Therefore, leaving the principles of the doctrine of Christ, let us go on unto perfection; not laying again the foundation of repentance from dead works, and of faith toward God. (Hebrews 6:1 KJV)

Triumphants further believe in the life-after-death spirit of victory as written about in 1 Corinthians 15:14: "And if Christ has not been raised, our preaching is worthless, and so is your faith."

Believers accept that Ye'shua was a man of flesh and blood chosen by the spirit of God to be a human voice teaching man God's desires and ways. We believe he was anointed and ordained by God to be the mediator between God and man. Triumphants believe as declared by modern theologians that Ye'shua was not God. Paulus (1761–1851 in Strimple 1995) declared that Yeshua's mission was to cause the moral character of those in the day of Yeshua's teaching to be more in accord with the way of God. According to Paulus, Ye'shua, the man, knew what man needed to do and how he needed to live to reestablish the relationship between him and God. Believers accept the thoughts of Paulus.

The Holy Spirit had revealed to Ye'shua the power and ability that man (Jews) had over his life, world, and affairs. Ye'shua was to teach man— those who would become believers because of his teachings—regarding that power and ability. He was to make them aware of the power he had to be victorious in all that would confront him. *In Modern Research for the Real Jesus* (1995), Strimple wrote,

> Jesus appropriated to himself everything in the Jewish messianic idea that was worthy of God and fulfilled all that in his holy religion of love as the spiritual Son of God. Jesus was even willing to die as the Messiah so that his death would win a higher messiahship as the Son of Man.

In the gospel of the kingdom era, Yeshua's life and death were the hope of redemption. Paul's effort was aimed at making early Christians aware of the teachings of Ye'shua and his disciples.

> If our hope in Christ is for this life alone, we are to be pitied more than all men. (1 Corinthians 15:19 KJV)

> And as we have borne the image of the earthy, we shall also bear the image of the heavenly. Now this I say, brethren, that flesh and blood cannot inherit the kingdom of God; neither doth corruption inherit incorruption. Behold, I

shew you a mystery; we shall not all sleep, but we shall all be changed, in a moment, in the twinkling of an eye, at the last trump: for the trumpet shall sound, and the dead shall be raised incorruptible, and we shall be changed. For this corruptible must put on incorruption, and this mortal must put on immortality. (1 Corinthians 15:49–53 KJV)

We shall be changed from mortal to immortal!

We have been given time to learn about him by getting to know ourselves. God is no respecter of persons. We, his creation, have the power to do all and exceedingly more than the Messiah did.

The things that I [the messiah] have done must you do and even greater. (John 14:12)

You have not cried in vain. Your … weeping has endured for a night but joy [will] come with the dawning light. (Psalm 30:5 KJV)

Our new day is dawning. Stay the course, hold to the prophecies, learn of him and who you are in him, and make ready for the new day and the new you.

If you are interested in learning more about the teachings of Triumph, you can find a Triumph the Church and Kingdom of God in Christ close to you. Visit it on any worship day. If you desire, you will be taught how to convert from being a Bible-only Christian to a Bible-based and revelation-structured believer. With others, you will learn the principles and doctrine that will empower you to conquer your weaknesses, fears, and doubts. As it was told to me many years ago, Triumph will make living a beautiful experience.

If you become a member of the Triumphant family, that does not mean you will not experience hardships; you will, but your faith in the doctrine and principles will empower you to withstand them and be strengthened. It will propel you beyond the limits of your humanness. Your view of your life will change; your hope of eternal life will look different. Becoming a member of the triumphant family will enable you to take another look at what you have believed and go beyond it to something greater. Eternal life is a reality; some will live rather than die. Some will be changed while living in their bodies, and that someone could be you. Decide today to focus on living a transformed life in a transformed world.

CHAPTER 5
MAN AS GOD-BEING

We are so much more than we know. We have denied ourselves the benefits of our reality. We are God's image of himself. We are the manifestation of the idea of God-being. God lives and moves in us. God is the divine force moving through the universe in various forms of life— animal, plant, and human—you and me, bodies of flesh housing all divine energy that supersedes all other forms of life. We have a connection with all other forms of life that they do not have with us. We have the power of being the I Am that can speak to the mountains of undesirables in our lives and move them from our path. We have the I Am power to walk over hot coals and not faint and run through mazes of confusion and not get weary. We have the I Am power to mount up as on the wings of an eagle and fly above suffering and disease. We are the I Am that can command the moon, the sun, and the stars.

As we are composed of the energetic force known as God, we can speak peace to the storms and call light out of darkness. As the God I Am, we are endowed with wisdom, the bread of life we can feed the hungry with. The love of God in us is so powerful that it can uplift the downtrodden. Grace and mercy revealed through us can heal the sick because sickness is just a thought of the unenlightened. The power of God in us can raise the dead for there is no death, just life unawakened.

As the spirit of the I Am God, we have the power to bring forth the heavens for heaven is a thought in the minds of the sons of life; we can set captives free, open the eyes of the blind, unstop the ears of the deaf, and make the lame walk and the dumb to talk. We are the power being God I Am. We are whatever we perceive God to be. There is no savior greater than the I Am that is you and me. There is no sin other than the darkness, the ignorance of one's own mind. We are the light, we have the knowledge; therefore, we must let our light shine, let it shine, let the God I Am in us be forthright so darkness (ignorance) cannot understand it. Be the light. "If [anyone] lacks wisdom, let him ask ... that he may know" (James 1:5).

Would a wise God have only one man deliver his message of truth in a particular time and leave others who came later to have only a translated— correct or not—version of his message as the only Word? The preachers would not have the Word from God that they preach but only a scripture from the book of scriptures. Where then would be the Messiah for us today? Should we worship Ye'shua or teach solely from the recordings of those teachings and not worship or praise God, the Father of created life and living? God has a voice for all seasons, and he has a voice for us today. God still reveals himself to anointed, ordained ones so that we may know His will.

One of the most powerfully spiritual messages of this day came through the revelation and vision given to Apostle Smith. The mantle was passed from him to those who would preach the message then and empower those who preached the message of the incarnated God and living eternal life. That message is still a living one spoken from the mouth of living messiahs. We are not limited to worship and prayer or going through the name of Jesus, Ye'shua, Immanuel, Allah, Elohim, Jehovah, or any other name to commune with God the Father.

> We have been given the power to become the son(s) of God. (John 1:12 ESV)

> Therefore, He who has an ear, let him hear what the Spirit says to the churches. To the one who is victorious, I will grant the right to eat from the tree of life. (Revelation 2:7 KJV)

And he said unto them, He that hath ears to hear, let him hear. (Mark 4:9 KJV)

The privilege of communicating with, worshipping, praising, and praying to God is our divine right. Ye'shua, the one anointed by the divine spirit of God, said we could pray to the Father ourselves because the Father loved us. If we could understand our beingness, we would understand that when we pray to the universal God spirit, we are praying to the I Am who we are. We are spiritual beings manifesting in bodies because we are beings in a time of manifestation. All things are being manifested; therefore, to be in this space and time, we must be as it is where we are in manifested bodies experiencing life as substance. Regardless of what we see ourselves as through the eyes of this manifest body, the reality of what we are is still spirit. Our bodies are physical, but we are spiritual.

That which hath been born of the flesh is flesh, and that which hath been born of the Spirit is spirit. (John 3:6 KJV)

We can call ourselves the cloned image of our Creator. All of this was verified when the Messiah said, "When you see me, you see the father" (John 14 KJV). The Messiah taught spiritual things because that is what he was. He could teach only what he was given to teach.

If I tell you of earthly (familiar) things and you believe not, then you will not believe if I tell you of heavenly (spiritual) things. (John 3:12 KJV)

He admonished us to "seek that we may find" (Matthew 7:7 KJV). He finished his work; therefore, he will not come back to do again what he finished before he left the world in his bodily form. The Messiah is not the object of worship for Triumphants, true Believers or those seeking to go higher. We worship the universal, divine spirit of creation, the Father of all life. Through the spirits of triumph, life, and living, we are quickened into the realm of everlasting life where all possibilities are revealed. God said in Isaiah 42:8 (KJV), "I Am the Lord, that is my name! and my glory will I not give to another, neither my praise to graven images."

Christ works through the Holy Spirit to quicken our mortal minds so we would be constantly reminded of the reality of our being—who and whose we are—and the power there is in knowing. Oh, how different our lives would be if we only knew and understood the reality of our being, if we only knew the I Am is the I Am who we are.

CHAPTER 6
BE YE TRANSFORMED

Whatever you thought you had to do to worship God, find favor with him, or praise him, you don't have to do that any longer because "former things are come to pass and new things [have been] declared." A transformation has already begun in you. You have become curious about what you have heard about God and man. You are thus a chosen one. The way you were before is now in the archives. You are becoming a new creature. Your spirit is expanding in you. The words of a song revealed to Bishop Crawford, which we sing, are "My thoughts are being corrected, my mind is being perfected"; it is an indication that a change is taking place in you. When you begin to seek, you will find. What you find may not be what you thought it would be if you had any thoughts about what you would find. If you ask for knowledge and understanding, be ready for something that will perhaps blow your mind. God works in you through the power of the Holy Spirit, and God works wonders. There is a new world waiting for you to explore. There is new life waiting for you to live. There is more joy waiting for you to experience and more God waiting for you to know.

To enter that new world, you must make a change. You must "be transformed by the renewing of your mind." You must develop a new way of seeing, thinking, and living.

> And I saw a new heaven and a new earth, for the first heaven and the first earth had passed away (Revelation 21:1 KJV)

When we allow the Holy Spirit, the spirit of triumph, life, and living, the spirit of the infinite one, the I Am in us to quicken and transform our minds, our old heaven and old earth will pass away. When a change takes place within, everything without also changes.

> And God shall wipe away all tears from their eyes and there shall be no more death, neither sorrow nor crying, neither shall there be any more pain; for the former things are passed away (the way it was is not the way it will be in the new world.) And he that sat on the throne said, behold I make all things new. Read Revelation 21 (any version).

> The throne John spoke of is not a structure of wood and ornament; rather, it is a concept in divine consciousness. It is where the spirit of God, the I Am, reigns.

The way of triumph is a freeing power for new-world worshippers. We do not need any other God Son to speak on our behalf. Those who have the awareness of the Holy Spirit have been given power to be called the sons of God, to execute the I Am power. Today, those who have heard the Word revealing the newborn sons of God can claim their divine right to God's miraculous power. They have the power to cast out demons (poisonous messages that keep them and their people perishing from lack of knowledge). The reformed, newborn children of God have the power to roll away the stones that block the resurrecting power of the Holy Spirit in them and their people. These are his anointed sheep of his pasture. The shepherd is admonished to feed his sheep. God is Lord and Savior, and he will not give his glory to another.

Ye'shua is no longer the light of the world; however, the light is not dimmed. He passed the mantle to his disciples. We are endowed with the power to light up the world because he made us one with him; we are now the light that illuminates the darkness of a sinful world. The Word of God in us is the fuel that keeps the light burning. "Ye are the light of the world"; therefore, "we" and we alone "must let our lights shine" (Matthew 5:14) and light up the new world beginning with ourselves. We must not trouble ourselves; if we waver between God and Jesus, we will remain in a sick consciousness because we are double-minded, and a double-minded man is unstable. Wavering between the Father and the Son leaves us powerless to do the work of either spirit, for "ye cannot serve two masters" (Matthew 6:24 KJV).

> Behold, the tabernacle of God is with men, and he will dwell with them, and they shall be his people, and God himself shall be with them, and be their God. (Revelation 21:3 KJV)

> He that overcomes shall inherit all things; and I will be his God, and he shall be my son. (Revelation 21:7 KJV)

Ye'shua said that the Father was in him. He is in us, and we are one. Through the Son, we are one in the Father, Son, and Holy Spirit.

Look at what you believe and follow. The way that leads to destruction of the peace, joy, health, prosperity, and happiness in you is broad because there are many on that path grabbing at what is easy to grasp. It is always easy to follow the crowd, to do what everyone else is doing, and to go where everyone else is going. If you do not have to lead the way or make the rules, it is easy just to go along with the way already paved, follow the established rules, and pray for the outcome you desire.

There is a way that seems right to man. The mind of man is gullible, vulnerable, and absorbent as a sponge. But then it analyzes what it has absorbed. The idea of another spirit new to the world of the chosen ones is difficult for it to accept. For example, the name of Jesus has been prominent for over 2,000 years even though there are a multitude of reasons why we should not remain loyal to the object of familiarity. Remember, the man called Jesus finished what he came to do and upon departing gave his power to those he left behind. However, it is difficult for the human mind to absorb something new and different. For example, the concept of God incarnated in man along with the concept of living without experiencing physical transition. The conscious awareness of the quickening spirit of life and living is a difficult concept for the human consciousness to absorb. It is the spirit that will project you from the binding loyalty to the familiar into the freeing acceptance of the new.

The familiar concept says you will live in your body for years, struggle to survive, experience sickness and disease, and be despondent. There will even be times when you will despair. For most of your life, you will know only limited peace, joy, prosperity, and happiness, and then you will die and find total fulfillment in heaven in or beyond the sky. It is easier to accept that concept than it is to accept the one that assures that by way of the new and unfamiliar, it is possible to live in peace and joy free from sickness and suffering, disease, despair, and despondency and believing you can overcome, subdue, and conquer whatever you experience.

The message and doctrine of new-thought revelations such as the revelation from which the institute of Triumph has come, such as the teachings of the Infinite Way and other revealing New Thought teachings, must be understood and accepted. Acceptance will release the power of the indwelling Spirit, which will begin to transform the consciousness of familiarity. The idea of heaven will begin to be realized and experienced while life still lives in the body.

When the Holy Spirit begins to work in your consciousness, your God-self, the I Am you are will begin to manifest itself in your life. The active spirit will cause the man self to lose its identity as one who must suffer the turmoil of human living. The Holy Spirit begins the transforming work of awakening the God spirit in you so your concept of life and living will change. The human consciousness begins to connect with the incarnated spirit of God, the spirit life in you. The two come together as one. God in you and you in God are formed by the divine wisdom, intelligence, and power of the supreme, everlasting spirit. Your divine body was made to house the divine spirit of life—forever.

CHAPTER 7
SPIRIT LIFE

M an can live beyond the limited number of years the human mind has accepted. Research is proving in many instances that the sickness and disease man accepts is not fatal and can even be eradicated through the process of mind transformation and some lifestyle changes. Many advances have been made in the unfamiliar that supports the doctrine of triumph. Once, it was accepted without question that death was inevitable. It is now being taught and accepted that God and man can live as one in the body conquering all.

Some are embracing the doctrines and principles of these teachings, and others are finding the subject of living something worth taking another look at. In *Three Magic Words* (Andersen 1954), there is much that supports the teachings and principles of life and living. It was revealed to the late Apostle Smith that God and man can live together—God in man and man in God. Andersen said in his foreword (page 8), "Man is not body alone ... Man is spirit, clearly and without dispute." Spirit is without substance; therefore, it cannot break down, get sick, suffer disease, or die. The destiny of man as spirit is to live as spirit being as man—pure, perfect, whole, and complete in a divinely designed body.

Man has determined that after a few years of journeying through his humanness, he will die, go to heaven, and live again in splendor with God, Jesus, and all those who have lived and died along with the angels.

Somewhere along the journey, man forgot about his creation, how he was born of spirit by spirit and came forth out of spirit. Regardless of the body, which houses the spirit-born spirit, the spirit is still undefiled spirit.

The spirit was designed to continually renew itself. It's said that every seven days, every skin cell has been renewed, that every forty-five seconds, all blood has circulated throughout the body, that the heart beats over 100,000 times a day, and that humans are able to live for over two hundred years (Kowalski 1992, "8 Steps to a Healthy Heart"). Today, many wonders are being revealed about our bodies, which can heal themselves if they are properly cared for. Just recently, it was reported that if we keep our thoughts pure, good, and positive and in a state of praise and thanksgiving, that will keep our bodies free from sickness and most diseases. When it comes to this thing called life, we must reexamine our concept of what everlasting life means. We must take another look at the information we are receiving about our bodies and take another look at the studies being conducted regarding human life. In Isaiah and Revelation, God said he would create a new heaven and a new earth, so the earth as we know it is not necessarily the earth where the new life will be lived. We must keep our ears and eyes open to behold the changes that are taking place and will take place. Everything will change as our consciousness changes. When our minds have been renewed, the world will be renewed. See God everywhere in everything, and "let this mind be in you which was also in [the Christ]."

In *The Immortality Factor* (2002), author B. Bova talks about the possibility of doing what before now has been declared unlikely, even impossible, overcoming all obstacles, every part of the brain, nerves, mind, and cellular structure completely renewed, changed to live in the changing environment despite the obvious acceptance of sickness and death. Immortality is a reality. It is not only probable but also possible, and for Triumpians and New-Thought Believers, it is a promise John the Revelator saw coming from God. Many are called, but only a few are those who have chosen to renew their minds. It is no mystery that life is to be lived forever. In the beginning, life was made to live as its Creator lived—from everlasting to everlasting.

The argument pertaining to immortal life is made between modern man and the idea of Ye'shua. There is much discussion about the return of the man Ye'shua. It is said that he gave up his life so that man could live free from sin and live forever with him in heaven, where the gates are pearl, and the streets are gold and we all will just walk around all day. Ye'shua, as we know of him did not come on the pages of history until the fourth century, and every healing, lesson, and miracle and his crucifixion, death, burial, and resurrection had occurred by the first century by the first messiahs (Singer 1906). Just as is the misinformation about Jesus/Ye'shua, an enlightened and anointed man, the deliberate misappropriation about his identity, life, and being is the truth about ourselves.

The spirit of truth and wisdom is here to ensure that the human mind is awakened to its reality, its I-deity. The message of the triumphant way of life is a main source of truth and wisdom. It comes as a quickening power. All who adhere to the working of its power will be projected beyond all sickness, suffering, and lack. These thoughts strive in darkness and hide in the depths of the subconscious. They linger there until a transformation begins: "Be ye transformed by the renewing of the mind." The spirit in the powerful message of divine truth acts like a slingshot. It holds your mind in the ready position until the time is right. When the man mind realizes that it does not have to make all the stops along the way, it releases the sling and projects the mind beyond the stimuli that cause the manifestation of negative circumstances. New-world messages and lessons are catalysts for change. Are you ready for a mind renewal, for a transformation of life and living?

CHAPTER 8
A QUICKENING SPIRIT

Just as the first-century Messiah, Ye'shua, brought a quickening, electrifying, enlightening message to the chosen ones of his era, as the Holy Spirit was a quickening, electrifying power of the apostolic era, so the spirit/message of revealed new thought/new world teachings are quickening, electrifying power for the chosen ones of this day.

The revealing spirit of today works with, in, though, and by the Holy Spirit to work the work of He who sent It. It is the spirit, the essence of the Allness of God. We are the receptors of what the Holy Spirit and the spirit of the new world give for the salvation of all men. Man, who has been transformed by the quickening power of the Holy Spirit, is the I Am of the divine, supreme, creative spirit of all life. We are God, the I Am. Therefore, we are perfect. Declare it and be it.

The Infinite Way, the established work of Joel S. Goldsmith, contains information that will open your mind to thoughts of infinite life and living. The Infinite Way studies will also cause a renewing of the way you think. It will open you mind and change the way you think about living a triumphant life for infinity.

Both the teachings of Triumph and the Infinite Way will reveal that the physical body and mind are perfected by the quickening power of the Holy Spirit. The teachings of those teachings will reveal that perfection in you is that inner part of you that is your I-deity, your perfect God-Spirit being.

As spirit, you, the God of your being, can adapt to universal changes. Your spirit being must embrace you as the body of flesh you are and quicken it into Itself whereby the two—spirit and flesh—become one. The body and mind becoming one consciousness, one being, must become one Being. One identity must become its I-deity – its reality.

Unless the spirit of life and living is active in and through man and converts him, he will ultimately perish, for everlasting life is in the consciousness of the indwelling spirit, not in the flesh consciousness. You must take another look at your reality. Your salvation comes when you realize that you are spirit, you are the realization of God, all that God is and as such you have power to do or be that manifesting on earth.

The status of the world's behavior in the church and the secular world is swiftly spiraling downward in disbelief and destruction. That downward spiral is enough to motivate those chosen by God for this day to actively seek the truth that will awaken sleeping minds. Those who have been anointed with an iota of understanding must accept the responsibility of shouting with a voice of triumph to alert the people of the need to awaken to a new truth.

We can no longer remain in a state of complacency. Status quo is no longer acceptable. We must be in hot pursuit of the liberating truth, the quickening power that will transform the hot or cold or those remaining asleep. (Read Revelation 3:15–16).

Truth empowers you to conquer all you will be confronted with along this journey. You and all seekers of truth must be fully awakened by the quickening power of the Holy Spirit.

CHAPTER 9
THE QUICKENING POWER

Yeshua's teaching was to awaken the Jewish people of that day to their reality and to free them from the binding, archaic, Old Testament laws. He became aware of the anointing that was upon him. He was aware of his spiritual power, but he had to learn to use it (Strimple 1995). In many instances, he used that power to show people their ability to use the power of their faith. One example is in John 5:2–8 (KJV).

> Now there is at Jerusalem by the sheep market a pool, which is called in the Hebrew tongue Bethesda, having five porches. In these lay a great multitude of potent folk, of blind, halt, withered, waiting for the moving of the water. For an angel went down at a certain season into the pool, and troubled the water: whosoever then, first, after the troubling of the water, stepped in was made whole of whatever disease he had. And a certain man was there, which had an infirmity thirty and eight years. When [the Messiah] saw him lying there and knew that he had been there a long time, said unto him, "wilt thou be made whole?" The impotent man answered him, "Sir, I have no man to put me in the pool when the water is troubled; while I'm moving toward the water, another steps down

into it before me. (paraphrased). The [Messiah] said unto
him, 'rise, take up your bed and walk."

Ye'shua did not touch the man; his spoken word did. He recognized
that same spirit in the man and appealed to it. That same spirit is appealing
to the indwelling spirit in man every day. Because of that indwelling spirit,
you must not surrender to the limited effects of your mind. Of itself, it is
unable to project you to the heights of victory. The victory for you is to
allow God to empower your mind to take up its limitations and walk into
the awakened consciousness called victory.

In Matthew 9:6–8, Ye'shua used his power again to appeal to the spirit
in another. A sick man was brought to him to be healed. Ye'shua did not
touch the man physically but spoke to the spirit of the man and told it to
"arise." The words he used caused the people to criticize him. He told the
man that his sins were forgiven. In my revelation, sin is ignorance—The
wage of sin is death ... My people perish for lack of knowledge. Lack
of knowledge signifies not knowing the God who empowers you to be
victorious. The man was being forgiven for being ignorant of his inner
spirit wherein was his power to conquer all. Matthew 9:6 (KJV) says, "But
that ye may know that the Son of man has power on earth to forgive sins."
He said to the sick man, "Arise, take up your bed and go." The man's spirit
was quickened and caused his mind to be lifted above its awareness and
acceptance of the conditions of his mortality. His God spirit was made to
realize its own power and the ability to use it. Thus, the sick man's mortal
mind rose to its own reality—unlimited ability. It then would not accept
or recognize conditions such as sickness, disease, lack, or limitations.

The God mind resurrects the mortal thoughts above its suffering.
Matthew 9:9 (KJV) says, "But when the multitude saw it, they marveled,
and glorified God, which had given such power to men." To men, not to
just one man. Even then, it was recognized that man was much more than
he thought. Somewhere, man has forgotten his original genetic anatomy;
he was made in the image of God. Man is now and always has been spirit.

Messages such as those of Triumph will quicken the mortal mind
of today's chosen ones and empower it to pick up its limited conscious
thoughts and walk in the newness of life. It will resurrect the mind into
the realm of spirit.

In your God mind, there are no thoughts of mortal circumstances. Quicken into the new mind, where Christ reigns, and be projected into the realm of consciousness, where God reigns. Be made whole, overcome, rise, and live.

In the resurrected mind empowered with wisdom and power of the Christ spirit, mortal thoughts will be changed. When your mortal mind is changed, you will be in a state of consciousness that is the dwelling place of the Christ spirit—God individualized. It is there to lead you into your God consciousness. That place is where you must go to be in the secret place of the "Most High" and to abide under the shadow of the Almighty.

The Christ spirit, the wisdom and power of God, the incarnated spirit of the new world, and the divine spirit of life and living working in you are the touch you need to become empowered to come out from your mortal thoughts and see a new world of spiritual peace, joy, love, grace, and mercy. You are ready to walk into the new world. Your mind will be in the realm where mortal conceptions have been changed. That new world, the renewed way of thinking, is where you must reign. This is the new world your resurrected spirit has created for you; rejoice and be glad in it. All things have been made new, and what is working in you is manifesting on the outside. Your testimony has been changed. You can now sing, "I see a new world for me."

As your transformed consciousness is being developed, you must not fret because of the limitations of mortal conceptions of the world. They are yet in their sins and yet remain in the dark. Even among us are some who are not sure of their search for infinite living just as we were. These are identified as Gentiles. In the Gentile world, the mortal mind can conceive of infinite life, but it is more difficult—nearly impossible—for it to conceive of infinite living because they believe in and are taught that there is something outside them that works the work that they can and should do for themselves. As you think ...

CHAPTER 10
SEARCHING FOR LIFE

As has been said previously, the search for infinite, eternal living is not exclusive to, for example, Triumph's way of life. Professors, philosophers, doctors, astrologists, and scientists are seeking the answer to the mystery of eternal, infinite living in this world in these bodies. Many strides are being made to prove what a man such as Apostle Smith presented to the world over a hundred years ago—Man is spirit, and as spirit, he is subject to life, not death.

Through the process of minds transformed and souls perfected by divine truth, the flesh-and-blood body will be redeemed and manifest as one with the spirit, which is the life of it. It will claim its rightful place as the third part of the new-world Trinity—Father, Son (in us and we in him), and Holy Spirit together in one and as one. There we are—one in the oneness of the trinity of spirit, soul, and redeemed body.

Ezekiel 18:31–32 (KJV) reads thus.

> Cast away from you all your transgressions, whereby you have transgressed and make you a new heart and a new spirit: for why will you die? ... For I have no pleasure in the death of him that dies said the Lord God: wherefore turn yourselves and live.

Why then does man die? The revelation for the new world has said that man can live eternally in his body, but only a few have chosen to hear it. The message has been recorded, the principles revealed, testimonies given, songs written and sung all following this revelation. Before life can live on in the fleshly body, man must rise from the bed of negativity, out of the pits of doubt. His soul must be cleansed of all thoughts of opposition to the idea of eternal life.

Only a few recognize that the spirit of God dwells in the soul of man. Man has the privilege of living as the God spirit in him lives. The mind of man must be completely transformed by the indwelling and universal, living spirit of truth—God. The earth must be prepared for the birth of the new man.

You must not just think that you can live; you must rise to the level of absolutely knowing that as the spirit of God dwells in you, you can live. You must know God, and since you cannot know God without knowing yourself, you must know yourself. I am that I Am. Knowing God and knowing self is a part of the at-onement. I am in God; God is in me; we are one.

The Genesis account of your oneness began when God said, "Let us make man in our image, after our likeness" (Genesis 1:26 KJV). After the likeness had been formed and life had been breathed into it, it became a living soul (Genesis 2:7). Man is one with his Creator according to Genesis 3:22 (KJV): "Man is become as one of us." It also implies that the man had the power to eat of the Tree of Life and live forever. Therefore, the idea of being one in and with God and the idea of living forever in the body originally created by the "us" in the beginning was revealed in the beginning.

You must know yourself as body and spirit. Your body was a thought in the "us" of creation and in your God mind. That thought shaped itself and came into manifestation forming itself around the mind, which thought it into being. Since the body was an idea in the mind of the spirit (consciousness), it was a perfect idea. The body's color, size, shape, etc., does not keep the life in the body from being perfect. If the mind of the body continues to entertain carnal thoughts, those thoughts will manifest themselves through the body—imperfect thoughts manifesting through an imperfect body. It does not fit with the perfect idea of the Creator.

Therefore, the misinformation of perfect in imperfection begins to show as sickness and disease and ultimately decay and death.

Eternal life is the natural inheritance of the perfect of which and in which you are included. The late U. S. Andersen wrote in *Three Magic Words* (1954),

> Your body is an embodiment of life, an expression of life, for through your body your spirit expresses Itself ... Your body is perfect even as the spirit within it is perfect. Only misuse of the spiritual law and what is identified as "error thinking" can take it from its state of perfection.

Since you are perfect spirit, you are entitled to all that is spirit including living eternally.

You are consciousness, consciousness is life, and life is eternal. The spirit that created you lives from everlasting to everlasting. You are the same as it. As life consciousness, you are eternal. Consciousness expresses through your body as the life of your body. Before there was a body, there was consciousness, which shaped and formed you as you evolved from idea to reality. It was so from the beginning, and it is so now.

We are all powerful. What causes our power to be effective is faith. No matter how powerful or wise we are, if we do not use faith, if we do not believe, the power is useless. We are wise. Our divine spirit knows all, and it knows when to use what it knows and how to use it. We must believe in that wisdom and have faith beyond the limitations of our human thoughts and understanding. The divine spirit knows all that is to be known.

The divine spirit is all knowing, all wise, and all powerful. What is in it is in you because you are spirit, and it is available for your use all the time. You are the manifestation of all that God is. In the mind where Christ dwells, think on God and the things of God and your mortal thoughts will be converted. In your mind, consciousness, and spirit, the Christ mind produces godly thoughts. Christ—the spirit of wisdom and power—dwells in your spiritual mind, your consciousness, the mind of God in you. In your mind, all ideas are born perfect and divine for they are born in the mind of the perfect, divine spirit. Ideas are processed and become things according to the level of consciousness you have.

Nothing is impossible if you have the faith. You can be free of sickness, disease, lack, limitations, and even death. Napoleon Hill (1937) wrote, "Whatever the mind can conceive and believe, it can achieve and receive," and that includes divine health and eternal living. In John 14:19 (NIV), Ye'shua said, "Before long, the world will not see me anymore, but you will see me, because I live, you also shall live." He did not specify that life would be for a season and then no more. The disciples were promised life beyond death. To understand this, you must spend time with the spiritual disciplines of meditation, prayer, and study. The Holy Spirit will reveal the truth of the statement "Because I live you shall live also."

We can trust in the promise of a new life when we see God in his reality beyond the illusion of flesh and blood. We shall stand in awe at the miraculous and powerful realization of the revelation of the spirit living as man. The revealed messages, the prophesies come alive—no longer mysteries but realized. The words, when they become alive, live among us. Then shall we see one another as we really are. We are spirit, and we shall live with the living Word. This time, rather than the Word becoming flesh and dwelling among us, we shall be spirit and dwell with it in the new earth. What a day, what a time, what a joy it will be.

Can you imagine how you will feel when the manifestation of the divine truth in your consciousness is revealed? Your mind in its human form must be renewed before it can conceive of what it will be like when the truth is realized, when the I Am that is and has been from the beginning until then is fully manifested. "Let this mind be in you which was also in Christ" (Philippians 2:5 KJV).

What a day of rejoicing it will be when you utterly understand the principle thought of being in God as God is in you through the Son. The oneness is real. Take a mentally visual journey, be still, and know that this truth is the focus of your faith. It is what you are living for!

CHAPTER 11
KNOW THE POWER

Isn't it great to know that the power in you is there for you to triumph in all the ways of life and living? The God spirit wants you to live in perfect peace and health with an abundance of every good thing. It put the essence of itself in you, and it is still there. From the beginning, the original idea of man was perfect, wise, and powerful, and thus, in that image, the seed of life was created.

God is life and living, and what God is, you are whether you are enjoying the God spirit or not. You depend on your concept of yourself and God. If you believe God to be an old, colorless man with colorless hair and a long colorless beard living in the sky, you are living outside yourself and denying yourself all the benefits of being a son of God. How can you enjoy what you are if you are not aware of who you are?

Ye'shua said that he was born to fellowship with those with whom he communed and even to endure the pain and suffering he endured. All of what was to be enjoyed was enjoyed. All of what was to be endured was endured. All of what was to be marveled at was so done—the healings, deliverances, and resurrections, the enlightening, inspiring, informative, and challenging lessons, and messages—were done with joy, gladness, and acceptance because he knew who he was—the Messiah. He was being himself and did not spend any time justifying, criticizing, analyzing, or making excuses for himself. He knew that his identity was not as important as his I-deity. It was important that he relinquished his man self so the divine spirit in him and working through him would be the ultimate manifestation.

He knew who he was. He knew why he was doing what he was doing. How different it would be if you, also a divine son of God, knew as Ye'shua knew, "When you see me you see the father." He did not always realize his divinity and the power he had; the Holy Spirit anointed him at his baptism and continued to instruct him in his anointing. As he successfully completed the lessons of his divine nature and his studies in the temple, as he successfully taught and demonstrated the divine power in him and proved the effectiveness of faith in that power, he became the Christ. He had to demonstrate that power to the ultimate before the title of the Christ was bestowed upon him. He had the knowledge all the time, and he had the ability to exercise great wisdom and power, but he had to open himself as a human to the Holy Spirit's teaching and learn how to use it. He had to develop himself to the point of knowing what he knew and doing what he did when it was time to do so.

> For I have not spoken on my own authority, but the Father who sent me has himself given me a commandment— what to say and what to speak.[50] And I know that his commandment is eternal life. What I say, therefore, I say as the Father has told me. (John 12:49–50 ESV)

Regardless of all you know or your title in your church or school, you must spend time in the school of divine revelation learning business, science, cosmology, astronomy, planetology, math, history, etc. You must study to be an approved workman in the field. You must know the answers to the questions you will be asked, and you must know the questions to ask to get the answers that will reveal the truth you seek. That truth lies in the consciousness of all men, but the new-world messiah, the Christ man of this day, must know how to awaken it in seekers and how to recognize and demonstrate it in himself. The power to do and to be the divine creature you are is in you.

Two stories prove that divine power is in all men, and it can be used. The first story is about a man in India who planted an orange seed and covered it with his manila. In approximately forty-five minutes, an orange tree had come up complete with branches, leaves, and blossoms and within a few minutes more oranges. In the crowd around him were twelve people with cameras taking pictures of what the young man had appeared to have done. When one of those in the crowd attempted to pick an orange off the tree, there was no tree there. Later, when the films were examined, there was a tree pictured there. How could that be? The young man told them to meet him the next day right there.

The next day, the young man planted another orange seed, and the same thing happened. That time, no one attempted to pick an orange off the tree. Those who had been deceived the day before told a chief why they did not try to pick an orange the day before. The chief picked an orange off the tree and ate it, and the others did likewise. The tree is reported as still standing and bearing fruit (Spaulding vol. 5, 1955, 32–33).

The power is in you; you can use it whenever you need to. It is a privilege you were born with, and it was in you at creation.

The second story is mine. It occurred on a cold February day when a friend and I were celebrating the birthday of the man who eventually became my husband. We began the evening with dinner, fun, and laughter. For some reason, I had an allergic or chemical reaction to something. It lasted far into the night with my behavior being way out of character and quite frightening to my guests. Finally, the episode subsided, and I was escorted to bed.

The next morning, I was awakened by brilliant white light and the distant sound of my children's voices. They were ready for Sunday school and did not know why I was not. I heard them, but I could not respond. When they realized I was awake but unresponsive, they called an ambulance.

The EMT tried to get a response from me but could not find a pulse. I cried out, "I'm alive! I'm not dead!" The life consciousness in me was striving to be heard over the noise of common belief. I thought I was yelling, but it was all in my mind. The reality of life living was strong and powerful in my consciousness.

The ER staff did all they knew to do but were unable to get a response, so they pulled the sheet over my head and pushed my gurney against the wall. I do not know how long it was before a doctor came, lifted the sheet, and looked at the body lying on that gurney. Something in me quickened, and it yelled, "I'm alive! I'm alive!" The spirit of life was alive in me and was striving to be acknowledged.

I woke up with an IV in my arm. I was alive just as my spirit had proclaimed. When my spirit dropped down into the body lying in that hospital bed, I knew I was truly alive!

We have the power of life and death in us. God is omnipresent, and he abides in us. We need no lessons, no degrees, no special talents, or skills to use the power in us. All we need to do is accept the truth that the power is there. With our mustard-seed faith, God will work for us. We may not be consciously aware of his presence in us, but our minds know whence that power came, why it exists, and how powerful it is. It knows how to use it to work for us. We must accept it, use it, and give thanks for it.

According to Spaulding (1955, vol. 5, 34), if anyone anywhere has ever accomplished anything such as in the stories above, all have the same power, the same divine right and privilege. God is no respecter of persons; everyone has the power, which is omnipresent and works in every situation.

Divine wisdom, power, and knowledge are yours to use to achieve victory. There is no need for you to want for anything. It gives God pleasure to give you the kingdom (Luke 12:32). There is no need for you to fail at anything for in divine reality, there is no such thing as failure. You are a master who has been called out to use your unique power to bring about a change in your life, and that will testify of empowerment for others. You have been changed to be the son of triumph, of divine reality, and as an inhabitant of the new world.

Apostle Smith wrote,

> The last trumpet is the everlasting gospel (Christ) ... calling
> [you] from under the power and hands of [these] enemies:
> bondage of corruption, diseases, sickness and pain, death
> and the grave, out of mortal into immortality ..., into
> the eternal life of ... God." Yes, it is calling you out from
> all human institutions; out of human wisdom; out of all
> societies and so-called life insurances, out from the human
> ideas; out from the consciousness of the limitations of
> human ways. (*What We Believe and Teach*, second ed., 62)

Since you have been called to disconnect from these things, you should not still be following the dictates of the human consciousness and remaining bound to an identity you are unconsciously connected to.

When you awaken to your I-deity, your God-self, you will begin to live joyfully and enjoy the glorious life in a transformed mind and a redeemed body. This is the message for seekers of new-world truth, the message that the voice of triumph, the voice of new world, divine truth, has brought. This is the promise that the spirit of divine wisdom gives. When you accept this message and begin to live in accord with it, no raging storms or poisonous doctrine can penetrate your transformed mind; no sickness, pain, suffering, sorrow, and death will be able to destroy you.

You will never be anything other than the God-self you are. When you are redeemed and awakened to your reality, when you realize there will never be a time when God spirit is apart from you, when you realize that as you live, you live unto God, you will realize your oneness with God. Ye'shua said, "On that day you will know that I am in my Father, you are in me, and I am in you" (John 14:20 ESV).

Humanity has been influenced by carnal thoughts and limited understanding for far too long. Those thoughts and that understanding have formed in you the idea that you and God are separate entities and that only Ye'shua is one with God, but Ye'shua said, "Teaching them to observe all things whatsoever I have commanded you: and ... lo, I am with you always, even unto the end of the world" (Matthew 28:20b KJV).

The messianic message is insufficient for you if you are striving for a more prolific understanding and higher awareness of God in you. It has influenced you to believe that "Jesus" is your Lord and Savior now.

The teachings and new commandment of Ye'shua were to awaken the God consciousness of man. Yeshua's early followers saw him as their Lord and Savior. However, man can realize that the purpose of Yeshua's teaching was to transform man's thinking of himself as being weak, dependent, and a helpless being needing a savior and to make him realize that he had the power in him to rise above the helpless state of consciousness to the omnipotent state of being.

Man has thought of himself as being powerless and in need of something or someone outside of him to grant salvation. Ye'shua/Jesus said he had finished the work the Father had sent him to do: "I have glorified thee on the earth: I have finished the work which thou gave me to do" (John 17:4 KJV). Isaiah 43:11 KJV tells us that the Lord said, "I, even I, am the Lord; and beside me there is no savior." Why then is there a need for another savior? Visions and revelations have come to make you aware of your redemption. You are not in bondage except to your carnal thoughts and lack of divine understanding. When I look out on creation, I see the glory of God. When I see you, I see God. You are at your weakest when you look outside yourself for a master or for God. What you are looking for is in you already.

You might ask how you can make your inner power work for you. Well, the moment you accept as truth that divine power is yours, you set it free. When you accept the truth that you are endowed with divine power, wisdom, and knowledge, you are claiming your mastering power. Through fasting, prayer, and meditation, it will be revealed to you how to do greater works than those Ye'shua did.

As I see it, the Jews needed a savior on the other side of the cross. Ye'shua was born for the day in which he lived, and his purpose was to enlighten the Jews who had been under harsh law. He was born to be the Messiah of the world on that side of the cross. His lessons, his task was for his people, those chosen to be delivered by the message he brought— the good news of hope and freedom that would release them from the harsh law.

The Jews who had been imprisoned and enslaved by ignorance needed to know the redemptive power of love, and Ye'shua gave them that power. With the redemptive power of love, he showed them that love forgave, and that forgiveness healed. He taught them about the power of love that set captives free. He taught them about themselves. He empowered his disciples to build on the foundation he had laid. In Luke 10:19 (KJV), Jesus anointed them with the "power to tread on serpents and scorpions, and over all the power of the enemy: and nothing would [will] by any means hurt you." That era ended when that Messiah declared that his work was finished. He passed the mantle on to his disciples when he said, "I say unto you, He that believeth on me, the works that I do shall he do also; and greater works than these shall he do, because I go unto my Father" (John 14:12 KJV). The beginning of the new day began then, and it continues today in the land of man when inspired men such as Ben

Ammi, Apostles Elias Dempsey Smith, Daniel H. Harris, Robert Redding, Russell D. Clark, and men such as Apostle-elect Sylvester F. Steele Sr., U. S. Andersen, and Joel S. Goldsmith as well as Mothers Floretta Young, Johnnie Coleman, and Cora Brice and Dr. Elizabeth Atkins, to name just a few, came forth with revelations which provoked our thinking and projected us into another realm of spiritual enlightenment.

The instructions of Ye'shua to "go ye therefore and teach all nations" (Matthew 28:19 KJV) and Paul to do "those things, which ye have both learned, and received, and heard, and seen in me" (Philippians 4:9 KJV) are triumphant revelations of victory. I call them messages of life to show believers and seekers how to break the bonds of ignorance of God and man. It was foretold in Revelation 7:13–15 (KJV),

> What are these which are arrayed in "white robes?" and whence came they? ... These are they which came out of great tribulations; and have washed their robes and made them white in the "blood of the Lamb." Therefore, they are before the throne of God and serve him day and night in his temple and he that sits on the throne shall dwell among them.

White is the color of purity, of victory. Overcomers are arrayed in white (pure consciousness) because they have been projected beyond the consciousness of still being at the foot of the cross, where the stains of sin lie. They have been made pure (white) as they are no longer kneeling at the cross. They have been delivered and cleansed by the Word, which lived among them and dwelled in them.

Romans 12: 2 (KJV) instructs believers and seekers to "be not conformed to this world: but be ye transformed by the renewing of your mind, that ye may prove what is that good, and acceptable, and perfect, will of God."

Believers and seekers are in another realm of consciousness and do not have the same need as those who were first introduced to the delivering power of the new commandment of love have. Those who walked and talked physically with Ye'shua had a need to claim the actual blood for their deliverance; they had a need for the new message. They had a need for the Word that lived then as Ye'shua and was their salvation. That Word is alive to give hope to the lost, those caught in the net of doctrines and principalities of men in high places with no thought of divine inspiration. Those men were (and some are yet) concerned with controlling the thinking of people around them, people desperately seeking true revelations of the promise of eternal life.

The Word has come again to the chosen ones on this side of the cross as some believe in the revelation of triumph revealed to Apostle Smith in 1897. Only those who recognize they are endowed with the incarnated spirit can hear what the spirit is saying. When the troubles of this land and across the seas have ended, there is a new way of life and living. The revelation of triumph, life, and living, the spirit of the I Am having laid the foundation and opened the way to the new world, is the savior for today. It has revealed that the light of truth and wisdom in you is the delivering power.

This truth and wisdom are the blood in this new world of revealed truth. We recognize that Yeshua's shed blood was for the remission of sin, for the cleansing of the repentant believer. However, we do not have to be dipped in the water or washed in the blood because the Christ in us, divine truth, will deliver us from the sin of ignorance that has kept us and keeps us bound. Because of all he did then, we are free now. We have power to conquer the challenges in our lives now. Thank God for then and praise him even more for now.

CHAPTER 12
CHANGE OF LIFE

Man has gotten entangled in what has been considered the way of righteousness. He has envisioned himself as being in the green pastures of divine truth. That type of thinking has blinded him to what divine truth is—the Word of God living in the consciousness of man as his breath and life. The world has not heard and accepted the truth because it is entangled in the doctrine and principles of religion. Religion is not truth that will resurrect you to the higher level of consciousness you desire. You must be free from religiosity and materialism if you want to be in realm of truth. Truth is spiritual, not religious. Because God is spirit, those who seek him must do so in the spirit, in truth, not by being attached to the physical world.

Religion has been confused as the way to God and the ways of God. As it is, religion is what keeps man focusing on the politics of organized socializing in the name of worship. Ye'shua taught to judge not, yet in our religious organizations, rulers and leaders are placed after being judged worthy to be the leader of the organization or divisions of the organization. God's way is not the way of the world, and religion is not the way to God though it has been used to control man's thinking and behavior. Man has been told that he must give himself to God. How can that be when all souls (all life) already belong to God?

There must be a change in the way you think so you can be resurrected to the level of consciousness where you become aware of your oneness with God, the life in you. When you do, you are the manifestation of the spirit. Religion keeps you focused on material matters. It keeps your mind on the flesh and blood. You are in the material world, but you are not of it. You are spirit free to be, and you will be free when you allow the Holy Spirit to awaken your mind to the awareness of who, what, and whose you are. Arise, seeker, and wake up, believer! Be an overcomer!

In this world, you will have tribulations until you realize the truth of your reality. You are not a slave to anyone, any law, any doctrine, or any people. As a seeker, you are yet going through as you continue to seek freedom from religiosity, carnal-minded thinking, limited spiritual vision, and lack of divine understanding. During the dark days, it was acceptable to believe that life would be better when Jesus came back or when you died and went to live in heaven with him. That type of carnal-minded thinking enforced religiosity. Religious thinking remains and is enforced and reinforced by carnal-minded preachers, teachers, and other religious leaders. It is time for their thinking to change.

Oh, how blind are the eyes that will not or cannot see. The Lord said, "I have no glory in the death of the saints" (paraphrased from Ezekiel 33:11 KJV). Yet there are those who do not understand that they were created in the image and likeness of God. They have not been told that the Creator lives from everlasting to everlasting so that all will be empowered with the power to live.

> He will swallow up death in victory; and the Lord GOD will wipe away tears from off all faces; and the rebuke of his people shall he take away from off all the earth: for the LORD hath spoken it. (Isaiah 25:8 KJV)

Life will live in redeemed bodies in the glorified new earth or as it was in the beginning—a divine idea in universal consciousness, an unformed spirit. Life was created to live. Life is for living. Life is everlasting. It is spirit. It is your divine right by inheritance. A change is coming in the way seekers and believers are made aware of divine truth. The truth will not continue to be blended with false stories of glory based on the historical events of the past. The purpose of manifest man was and still is to glorify God. It is to let the reflection of the reality of God shine in the man created in his image and after the likeness of the us that brought it forth.

Yes, a change is coming. The truth about God, life, and living is being accepted by many who have been squashed amid stories told to prepare them for a life after death. Many are now looking at and listening to what is being told by doctors, researchers, philosophers, missionaries, evangelists, preachers, and others about the possibility of not physically dying. People still want to live in a land where there is no weeping and moaning, where evil deeds are no more, where true and unadulterated love is the order of the day.

People want to live without worrying if they will be accepted regardless of the color of their skin, nationality, race, education, creed, or anything else. People want to live without worrying about sicknesses, deadly viruses, and death.

The truth that has been uncovered tells us that we can look forward to living just that way. We can live and not worry about the things and conditions that have plagued the minds of humankind since the days of Cain and Abel. Today, we can look forward to overcoming every limitation that has prevented us from utilizing the power we have had from creation.

That time has not come into our reality yet. However, it is coming. John the Revelator saw that day coming. Others have also seen revelations of the day of the Lord coming. Researchers are working on proving it. Others have had dreams, and the vision has been revealed to chosen ones of God. Yes, there are those who have received this new-world revelation, this new-world message. Behold a mystery—All shall not die. All shall be changed. Before we can enter the new-world consciousness, we must be changed so we can live in it. The wisdom and power in the truth about who we are will enable us to be transformed. It will renew our minds and change the way we think and live.

You with your changed mind will be able to heal your body and prevent sickness or disease from plaguing you at all. You with your changed mind will live free from worry about being bound by ignorance of the divine truth. You will be free, empowered! Transformed! You will be able to overcome even death!

> Therefore, I say unto you, what soever things ye desire,
> when you pray believe that you have them, and you shall
> have them. (Mark 11:24 KJV)

The truth will bring about a change in the way you think, interact with others, and view your living experience. Once you begin to open your mind to this divine truth, you will experience freedom you have not felt before. You will feel you are in a new world. You will feel like a new you. This change will move you into a new way of interpreting the circumstances and situations in your physical, emotional, and mental lives. The divine spirit of life and living will be the catalyst for your interpretation. It will give you a spiritual understanding of the why questions you have asked about the happenings in your life.

The change you will experience will be the love, the agape love, the love that defies description and definition. That love will move you out of the shadows of uncertainty. It will enable you to see yourself and your experiences from a spiritual rather than a physical point of view. What the physical sees and attempts to understand is from an illusionary point of observation. It cannot see what the real outcome and comeback of physical activities are. Physical things are temporal illusions; they are a prelude to something else.

The spiritual observation will allow you to see beyond what appears in physical substance. It will reveal activities and circumstances that are prelude to what is to come: "Be not deceived, God is not mocked, whatsoever a man soweth, that shall he also reap" (Galatians 6:7 KJV). You may have thought that certain things occurred in your life because of luck—bad or good—but you will understand that your lifestyle or activities have produced the outcomes you are experiencing. As a man thinks ...

You can determine the outcome of your life by practicing love as the underlying factor in all you say and do. Love does not mean you agree with everything or everyone; it means that your observation of the circumstances and situations in your life are not to be viewed through your physical eyes; rather, you will understand that "to everything there is a season and a time for every purpose" (Ecclesiastes 3:1 KJV). You will love the idea that the God spirit in you will keep you thinking from a spiritual point of observation so that your mind will always keep you in an atmosphere of the good, the positive—the silver-lining point of view. Being renewed will transform your life and living and take you to the ultimate. This kind of thinking will keep your mind in a state of peace. It will bring joy, long-suffering, gentleness, etc. (see Philippians 4:8).

Love is the immutable law that will bring about the change that will move you toward the divine state of perfection, out of mortality and into the state of immortality.

CHAPTER 13
ETERNAL LIFE IS EVERLASTING

As a reformed thinker, you will have another Messiah, another truth, another message, another mission. Rather than looking back at what was, you must look at what has been given to you for your living today. In 1987 in a district conference, Apostle Robert L. Redding of Triumph the Church and Kingdom of God in Christ preached a message entitled "Investigate What You've Got." In essence, he said what I am saying here. You should take another look at what God has given you as a guide for living this incredible gift of life. He said that only a few really knew what they had and that most were just going along with the crowd.

According to Apostle Redding, you should be aware of the crowd because people will follow anyone if it seems he or she is going somewhere. He also said that before you start going along with the crowd, know where it is going, why it is going there, and what it will do when it gets there. That was eye-opening for me, and I often refer to his message.

This revealed message of Triumph is so much more than it is thought to be. It is a quickening spirit that will completely transform and redeem you. It will heighten your awareness of your oneness in the Trinity, into eternal life, into your God-ness, the I Am that you are. What more do you want? What more are you looking for? Are you so much like the people in the gospel of the kingdom era that you will turn from the gift God has given you? How long will you waver between opposing thoughts? Will you continue to move forward but look back? Will you continue to pine after what was rather than accept what is? Can you look forward to the new world John the Revelator saw coming and to what you will be?

The Holy Spirit working through new-world messages keeps beckoning you by its power, wonder, and might. It avails itself to you so that you can find yourself immersed in truth and conforming to this world but receiving the revealed truth from other authors and other sources so that you will feel assured that what we teach and believe is God-given truth.

Humankind is beginning to recognize what and where God is—life dwelling in us. We should be excited about each transformation we undergo at every level for it is taking us closer to mind perfection that will lead to body redemption, which will transition into the realm of eternal life. Eternal life will be manifested through a body as a being. This can be understood only as wisdom increases and consciousness awakens. The power of life and death is in us, in what we say and think. "Let this mind be in you that is also in Christ Jesus" (Philippians 2:5 NIV).

Be mindful of what you think and try meditating frequently. "Be still and know [that God is] God" (Psalm 46:10 NIV paraphrased). Be even more cautious about what you speak; your words have power and will bring into existence what you speak: "Thou shall decree a thing and it shall be established unto thee" (Job 22:28 KJV).

Conforming to the physical world will keep you from the path of righteousness, where you would receive the blessings of peace, love, health, prosperity, joy, and happiness. On the path of righteousness, there is nothing to keep you distracted and deaf to the voice of God. God has not stopped talking. He is yet feeding his flock. He is yet caring for his children. In his children's minds, he continues to be the wisdom, knowledge, and the understanding necessary for them on the path of righteousness.

God speaks his truth to open minds and receptive spirits. His principles and doctrines are directed by his voice. God's purpose is to empower believers with the truth that will make them free to live eternally. The gift God freely gives is eternal life. It is life to know God.

From everlasting to everlasting, God, the divine spirit of life, is omnipresent, omnipotent, and omniscient. Beloved ones, he is with you always—from everlasting to everlasting. You are governed by the eternal truth stemming from the reports of those who have witnessed it. You are guided by the testimonies of those who have been set free by his amazing grace. People literally die because they do not know they are the I Am, which they identify as God. They do not know how to accept him, apply his power, and follow his spirit, which dwells in them as them. They do not know God; it is eternal life to know God. We all have much to learn and understand about God and ourselves.

One night while I was watching TV, the screen turned completely white, and a drawing began to appear. As the drawing took shape, it began to reveal a crowd sitting around a table. At the head of the table was a vibrating light. When the drawing was finished, I asked, "Who are these, and why are they there?"

A voice spoke from the vibrating column of light: "They are waiting."

"What are they waiting for?" I asked.

"They are waiting to be taught," I heard.

"Who will teach them?" I asked.

"You."

"Oh no! Not me! I don't know what to teach them!"

"Yes, you! As I was with Moses, I will be with you. Teach my people to live and prepare them for life for my people are dying without knowing the joy of living."

"No, No!" I said. "I don't know how to live myself, so I can't teach anyone else how to live! No, not me! I can't do that!"

The experience was such a phenomenon that I cannot remember if it happened all at once or in a series of occurrences. I say that because even though the initial occurrence frightened me beyond my ability to describe, I testified at the weekly prayer meeting at church the following Wednesday. The pastor and congregation decided to sponsor me as a student at a seminary.

Ten years later, when I could no longer dodge doing what I had been commissioned and anointed to do, I was again challenged or rather commanded, "Teach my people to live, prepare my people for life, for my people are dying without knowing the joy of living. Teach my people to live."

That time, I surrendered, and in 1988, I was ordained by my district bishop. Since then, I have been endowed with astonishing information.

When I am teaching and preaching, information will come out of my mouth that amazes me. God is an awesome God, and he has never left me alone as I attempt to teach his people. God can never leave me, and he cannot leave you because we are one with each other, we are one with our God. We are manifestations of the God of our being.

> "For I know the plans I have for you," declares the LORD, "plans to prosper you and not to harm you, plans to give you hope and a future." (Jeremiah 29:11 KJV)

> Yet a little while and the world [will see] Me no more, but ye see Me. Because I live, ye shall live also. (John 14:19 KJV)

The divine spirit has created you and has given you mastery over whatever you will encounter during your transformation experience. You must triumph. You have control over yourselves and your worlds. As has been stated, that, beloved ones, is the key. You are the master of the experiences that will transform you. You must determine what it will be like and how long it will be. The divine spirit will accept whatever you determine.

> Ask and it will be given to you; seek and you will find; knock and the door will be opened to you. (Matthew 7:7 NIV)

The Holy Spirit works for you and will respond to your requests that are within God's will.

> Beloved, I wish above all things that thou mayest prosper and be in health, even as thy soul prosper(s). (3 John 1:2 KJV)

People have been lost in the darkness of ignorance far too long. The complexity of religious dogma has imprisoned their minds and left them feeling lost and without hope of finding the divine purpose for their lives. People have been looking for heaven and heavenly bliss in all the wrong places for they have journeyed outside themselves and have gone further away from their eventual destination. Eternal life is not just a phrase or something to be acquired further up the road. Eternal life is now; it lives in you, me—in all God's creation. Fret not yourselves, for there are some among you who will transcend physical death despite sickness, suffering, and trouble on every hand though death is tramping among you every hour of every day.

> Behold, I shew you a mystery; We shall not all sleep, but
> we shall all be changed, In a moment, in the twinkling of
> an eye. (1 Corinthians 15:51–52a KJV)

It is a divine truth that people do not perish from sickness, old age, disease, or suffering. People perish for lack of knowledge. It is written that "the wages of sin are death" and "My people perish from a lack of knowledge" (Hosea 4:6 KJV).

Armed with this information, you no longer need to look for God outside yourself for the answers to your questions about life and living. You do not have to remain imprisoned by ignorance.

Through Apostle Smith and other new-world writers, apostles, and teachers commissioned people of God, you will be kept aware of the plan of redemption in you and for you for this day. The plan of salvation includes freedom from ignorance. It ensures the establishing of the new-world vision. The wisdom of the triumph doctrine (teaching that reveals a spiritual way of life) is endowed with the empowering revelation of God. It is in the form of a new vison and enduring strength, authority, and devotion. It is a self-nurturing ability to conquer everything.

You have the power to squash death and live forever in your bodies that will have been transformed from mortal to immortal. What a revelation! The empowering spirit of God has been revealed; it is rooted in your soul (mind), and it is given for the redemption and salvation of those who will follow. No matter what you have done, have not done, no matter how lost you are or how low you may have fallen, God in you is the reality of you. Accept the truth that you are one with the Trinity—You are in the Son, the Son is in the Father, and the Father is the Spirit of life in us all!

CHAPTER 14
A NEW DAY DAWNS

You are standing on the edge of the horizon of the truth you may not have heard before. Fortunately, the flexible mind can expand to hold more knowledge than it can be exposed to. All that you are is consciousness, and all of consciousness is mind. Mind is spirit, spirit is consciousness, and consciousness is mind. Consciousness, mind, and spirit is the trilogy of what the real I Am is.

Now that you have a new view to consider—something to think about that will expand your conscious mind—you will experience living in a way you have never done before. I have talked about eternal life, consciousness, mind, spirit, doctrines, and principles; I have talked about not conforming to this world, about renewing your mind, and being transformed.

I have presented some new information and some you are already aware of, but one thing I have not talked about is the sealant that holds it all together—love. It is the greatest power; it transcends all circumstances and situations. You cannot talk about God or good, consciousness, or spirit without realizing that it all stems from and is rooted in divine love. God is love, and to know God is to know love. In 1 John 1 (KJV), we find a good biblical discussion about love.

> Beloved, let us love one another, for love is from God,
> and whoever loves has been born of God and knows God.

Anyone who does not love does not know God, because God is love. In this the love of God was made manifest among us, that God sent his only Son into the world, so that we might live through him. In this is love, not that we have loved God but that he loved us and sent his Son to be the propitiation for our sins [ignorance]. Beloved, if God so loved us, we also ought to love one another. No one has ever seen God; if we love one another, God abides in us, and his love is perfected in us.

So, we have come to know and to believe the love that God has for us. God is love, and whoever abides in love abides in God, and God abides in him. We love because he first loved us. And this commandment we have from him: whoever loves God must also love his brother.

Because we profess our love for God, we must also love God's creation. However, when we look at the evil, hatred, discrimination, sexual abuse, killings, divorces, human trafficking, greed, and all manner of discord in the world, we can find it hard to love unconditionally. Divine love empowers us to see the good, the God, in even the worst situations and circumstances. For God so loved us that he does not even consider our mischief, our sinfulness. As it is written, "Thou art of purer eyes than to behold evil, and canst not look on iniquity" (Habakkuk 1:13a KJV). As it is with God, so it must be with us! We are one with God; the activity of God is done through us as us.

When I was considering becoming a member of the triumphant family, I was impressed by the obvious love the members had for one another. Even after spending forty-six years as a member of the triumphant family, I still am amazed at the love its members demonstrate to and for each other. The love I experience in the triumphant family is the love that must saturate the atmosphere. We followers of Christ must show God's unconditional love to the world. The love of the people of God and the love of the teachings, principles, and doctrines demonstrated and taught by the people of God hold me firmly.

When we recognize our oneness with the divine spirit of God, which dwells in us and lives as us as we dwell in and live as the manifestation of it, we can see the truth in every situation. The universe is always in harmony with itself; everything has a purpose. If everything is in harmony with the universe and there is a purpose to everything, if all things work together for the good, there is no discord, and love is still eminent always. Love is God, God is love, and God is all there is.

We are to love one another after we learn to love ourselves. Love forgives all, so we are to forgive one another quickly and often. If we love, we will attract as our reward for loving the things associated with love. If we forgive what we ought to forgive, we will be forgiven when forgiveness is necessary ... And it always is.

The new-world revelation in which the message of redemption exists has come in word, in deed, and by spirit to take every nation of seekers and want-to-be Believers who desire to go to a higher level of wisdom, knowledge, and understanding of God and self. John the Revelator saw the new heaven and the new earth coming down. Apostle Smith, Goldsmith and others saw men living on earth in redeemed bodies without dying. Symbolically, heaven is the superconscious of man, and earth is his body. John further saw New Jerusalem (heart) coming down, which means that man's heart was being renewed and his consciousness was being prepared to enter the realm of eternal life to be lived in the new earth. Others have seen revelations relating to the eternality of life living consciously redeemed. This is triumph! This is victory! This is Spirit and Spirit is Life!

For a better understanding, find a Triumph Church or enlightened teachers who will study with you so that you will achieve a better understanding of the relationship between you and God and your right to eternal life.

> Study to show thyself approved unto God, a workman that need not to be ashamed, rightly dividing the word of truth. (2 Timothy 2:15 KJV)

Read the works of other enlightened, new-world writers including those mentioned in this book. Ask what you need to understand, seek what you need to find, and open your mind to receive what you need to receive to be resurrected to a higher level of consciousness of divine truth.

Finally, believe in the possibility of living in a body that is constantly being transformed and readied to live throughout eternity on earth that will be glorified by glorified believers. Believe in the eternality of conscious living. Life is consciousness (mind), and consciousness is life. Consciousness is forever. Believe in the eternality of consciousness (the mind). Believe in eternal life. Love unconditionally!

> Behold, I shew you a mystery; We shall not all sleep, but
> we shall all be changed. (1 Corinthians 15:51 KJV)

AND THUS, WE PRAY

Oh Lord our God who reigns supreme in the universe, we honor, worship, and magnify you in all your glory. We reverence you. You are the Father of all creation. We humble ourselves as we come before you and thank you for providing us an opportunity to live the incredible gift of life you have given us. We glorify you!

By the power of you as divine love abiding in us, our sicknesses are healed, our wounds are soothed, our brokenness is mended, and our diseases are erased. Our blind eyes are opened, and our deaf ears are made to hear. Stuttering is taken out of our tongues and limping out of our limbs. We have a song to sing and a testimony to share!

You are great and mighty, and you protect us from harm. Because of your indwelling presence, we can triumph in all our doings. Father God Jehovah, we glorify you!

For the blessings you have given, we thank you. For the privilege of coming before you in all situations, we thank you. For declaring your divine truth to all here on earth, we thank you. For your salvation, grace, and mercy, we thank you. For empowering us with wisdom and strength of endurance, we thank you. For all our over-comings, all our victories, Father, we thank you. For leaving us not alone and for leading us on the path of righteousness, we thank you.

For keeping our minds in perfect peace when all around us there is discord, Father, we thank you. For leaving us not alone in times when despair, despondency, turbulence, fear, and doubt plague our environment, when we are surrounded by the darkness that exists when your voice is silenced by the noise of emptiness, Father, when sickness, suffering, and internal struggles distract us from the peace there is in being consciously in your presence, holy Father, we give you praise.

Thank you for the security of being embraced by you and showered by your love. Most of all, almighty God, we praise and glorify you for Ye'shua, who showed us the gift and reality of eternal life you gave us.

That all may come into the knowledge of this divine truth, I pray that you will quicken the mortal minds of men and women everywhere. We give you, the omnipotent spirit of life, praise, and glory forever, amen.

BENEDICTION

No man cometh to the Father except by me. (John 14:6 ESV)

Christ speaks the same message to you. Your only contact with a master teacher is through the mastery in yourself. (Spaulding vol. IV, 1976)

May the illuminating light radiate in you. May the empowering love anoint you. May the invincible power of love divine surround and protect you wherever you are.

May the power of the almighty God bless and prosper you abundantly, and may you live a triumphant life conquering all the days of your eternal life. All hail and amen!

ABOUT THE AUTHOR

What I shared in this book began when I was growing up in Louisville, Kentucky. I remember being awed and curious about a woman who would walk down the street dressed in all white and being followed by her children. They would walk to a little white church down the block from the large Baptist church I attended. I was awed by the sound of the drum and tambourines that could often be heard coming from that church. I did not know that I would one day be a member of that group I was so curious about.

In 1968, my then husband and I and my two children relocated to a small coal-mining town in the Appalachian area of Kentucky. That relocation took me to a whole new exposure to life. To say the least, I was not prepared for the way of living I was about to experience. I was initially shocked. The lifestyle of the people there was strange to me and hard for me to adapt to, and their language was different. However, I eventually settled down and acquainted myself with the people and the environment. Many were the challenges, but I was accepted by the community, and I began to work with the children of the church and community. Nonetheless, however well I seemed to adapt, the challenges began to overwhelm me, and a significant change was about to take me on a journey I was not prepared for. Five years after a traumatic life, I found myself divorced and virtually alone with my two children.

Life there as a single mother was extremely hard. I had served the members of the church, but I and my children had to relocate again, only that time, I had no place to go.

At the time, I was attending the University of Kentucky Southeast Community College and had no job. I was not prepared to relocate. I reached out for help. One woman, who is now deceased, responded to my cry for help. She helped me with the children while I attended classes and looked for a place to live. With the help I received, I was able to complete my studies and serve as the first Black female student government president at my college. I was also appointed to serve as the president of the Intercommunity College Student Government Presidents of the University of Kentucky Community College system and to serve as a member of the Community College Advisory Committee. I graduated with an associate degree.

Soon thereafter, my children and I were blessed to be housed in a new and very nice apartment. Thanks to God and the way he works, I was able to provide for my children. We were surviving, but it still seemed as though I was losing all sense of direction and emotional strength.

It was during that time that I was introduced to the Triumph Church. All the time that I was struggling, Mother Newman (deceased), a local minister and shepherd, was praying, watching, and waiting for just the right time to introduce and invite me to come to the Triumph Church.

Mother Newman was the shepherd of the Triumph Church in that area. She was also our neighbor when we first relocated there. The little white church I had been curious about as a young girl was the same spiritual organization I was being introduced to. Its teachings, principles, and doctrines were different from those I learned at the Baptist church.

In the early 1970s, Mother Newman invited me to attend a conference at her church. I did not attend, but after one of the day sessions, she and Prince Robert Redding Sr. visited me and ministered to me. As that visit was coming to an end, Mother Newman made a comment that has stayed with me until this day: "Triumph will make a beautiful woman out of you if you let her."

One Sunday morning in 1973, after that memorable visit, I was on my way to the church I was a member of at that time. During the drive, I was preoccupied with my thoughts and driving remotely. It appeared as if the car were controlling itself. Without realizing it, I turned off the main road and crossed a little bridge onto the road that led to the Triumph Church. It appeared to stop on its own directly in front of the church. Puzzled as to how I had gotten there, I was in a daze trying to figure out what was going on.

I went into the church. It was dark inside, but there was a light shining in the front of the building. I walked farther into the church and toward the strange light. As I did, I discovered that the light was the sunlight reflecting off the headwear that Mother Newman was wearing. She was sitting alone, which was unusual, in the center of the church. I felt that whole experience was the spirit of the Lord guiding me to my new and a transformed life.

The following Tuesday, I attended the evening service and was put on the Prayer Roll. I did not understand at that time that being put on the Prayer Roll meant being received as a member in training. I would become a full-fledged member when I learned the governing doctrine and principles of the church and when my living changed accordingly.

For three years, I was on the Prayer Roll, but I continued to attend the Baptist church where I was a member. I also attended the Sunday night and weekly services at the Triumph Church. In addition to attending services six evenings a week, I was taught the principles of obedience and sacrifice by Mother Newman. Under her leadership, I learned the meaning of humility.

I began to live with a different outlook, a new perspective. I had a new zeal for life. Everything looked different. Life for me continued to be full of strange and mysterious happenings.

I continued to learn the doctrine and principles of the Triumph Church and how-to live-in accordance with them. The teachings were empowering and enlightening. I soon realized that I was changing ... I was adapting to a new way of life. I felt fulfilled. I felt empowered. I was shedding my Baptist consciousness and taking on the consciousness of a triumphant. I was learning what it meant to be a triumphant woman.

Under the teachings and living examples, my understanding of the doctrines and principles increased. Over and over, I was compelled to take another look at the changes taking place in my life. My life in and outside of triumph is a living testimony of what it means to overcome, subdue, and conquer whatever challenges may be. I love being a triumphant woman. I love this triumphant truth. I love this triumphant way of life!

—Elder Dr. Mary Rose Traylor

REFERENCES

Ammi, Ben. (1994). *Everlasting Life: From Thought to Reality.* Washington, DC: Communicators Press.

—————. (1990). *God, The Black Man, and Truth.* Washington, DC: Communicators Press.

Andersen, U. S. (1954). *Three Magic Words.* North Hollywood, CA.

Bova, B. (2002). *The Immortality Factor: How Science Is Expanding Your Life.* Pittsburgh: Tor Science Fiction.

Brice, C. A. (n.d.). *The New World Herald: Songs of Deliverance.* Pittsburgh: Triumph the Church and Kingdom of God in Christ.

Hill, N. (1937). *Think and Grow Rich.* Hollywood, FL: Frederick Fell.

Paulus, H. E. G. (1761–1851). In Robert B. Strimple (1995), *The Modern Search for the Real Jesus.* Phillipsburg, NJ: R&R Publishing.

Singer, I. (1906). Jewish Encyclopedia (2015): https:tbshamden.com/index.php? option.com

Spalding, Baird, T. (1955). *Life and Teachings of the Masters of the Far East.* Marina Del Rey, CA: DeVorss.

Strimple, Robert B. (1995). *The Modern Search for the Real Jesus.* Phillipsburg, NJ: R&R Publishing.

Triumph the Church and Kingdom of God in Christ. (1982). The Constitution of Triumph The Church and Kingdom of God In Christ. National Headquarters, Atlanta.